HUMOROUS COWBOY POETRY:
A KNEE-SLAPPIN' GATHERING

HUMOROUS COWBOY POETRY:

A Knee-Slappin' Gathering

SALT LAKE CITY

First Edition

98 97 96   10 9 8 7 6 5 4 3 2

Introduction copyright © 1995 by Gibbs Smith, Publisher.

Poetry copyrights remain property of individual poets.

This is a Peregrine Smith book, published by
Gibbs Smith, Publisher
P.O. Box 667
Layton, Utah 84041

Book design by J. Scott Knudsen, Park City, Utah
Cover art by Boots Reynolds
Dawn Valentine Hadlock, Editor
Madge Baird, Editor

Interior illustrations: Katherine Field, Fred Lambert and Lewis E. Wallis

Library of Congress Catalog-in-Publication Data
Humorous cowboy poetry / edited by staff members, Gibbs Smith,
    Publisher.
        p.   cm.
    ISBN 0-87905-658-4 (pb)
    1. Cowboys—West (U.S.)—Poetry. 2. Humorous poetry, American—
    —West (U.S.) I. Gibbs Smith, Publisher.
PS595.C6H86 1995
811.008' 03278—dc20   94-38117
                                               CIP

Printed and bound in the United States of America

CONTENTS

INTRODUCTION

One of the enviable perks of our jobs as editors here at Gibbs Smith, Publisher is the annual trip to Elko, Nevada, for the Cowboy Poetry Gathering. Each year we pull on our boots and duds to immerse ourselves in an art form that celebrates and savors the culture of the West. The Elko event is the granddaddy of similar gatherings that have sprung up all over the country and in Canada, too. Many of the poets represented in this collection hit the trail throughout the West, mostly at their own expense, just for the opportunity to share a laugh or a sentiment. Skinny Rowland, for example, is stricken with Lou Gehrig's disease and doesn't know how long he can continue performing, but says, "It will be as long as I can still stand up in front of a mike and make people laugh." Others perform locally, or not at all, content with the satisfaction of sharing their work with family and close friends.

Like the cowboys of old, these artists continue to preserve their culture through poetry and stories. And, like the old-timers, their ideas and inspiration come primarily from personal experience. It is not surprising, then, that some of those stories and poems are plumb full of humor—humor that comes, as cowboy Bob Court put it, "from being kicked, stepped on and thrown by a bunch of four-legged critics who have yet to appreciate my wisdom." For most, the ability to laugh at themselves and their situations is the dose of medicine that makes life tolerable at times.

When word got out that we were putting together a collection of humorous cowboy poetry, thousands of hilarious poems stampeded our way. Rounding them up and making a selection from those submissions was the most difficult task we've ever enjoyed! There were many poems we would have liked to include, but could not for the lack of space in the pens. But . . . there is always the chance of another roundup in the future, so hold onto your hats and keep your ears to the ground!

Perhaps the most enjoyable part of putting this book together was getting to know the cowboys and cowgirls behind the words. When asked for information about themselves, most of the poets expressed a deep respect and love for the land, the animals, the camaraderie of cowboys, and the freedom and values of their lifestyle:

"The freedom lets you think about God's creation, life's problems, and how they can all fit together for the good of mankind."
—Fred G. Ellis

"What I like best about ranching is the opportunity it affords families to work together. And I enjoy the brotherhood of cowboys."
—Virginia Bennett

"This type of lifestyle brings a person in touch with the most important values in life—integrity, industry, honest dealings with people, hard work, and total enjoyment of one's surroundings."
—David J. Ball

"The ranching game is a great experience. I love to be up in the morning when life begins to stir and to see the sun rise. The most enjoyable part of ranching is feeding stock in the wintertime and watching new birth and new growth in the spring."
—Jim Ross

These cowboys also voiced a desire to pass the legacy of the West on to their children and others, as it was passed on to them, through the cowboy oral tradition. Drawing from personal experiences, old stories and jokes, conversations (especially with older cowboys), history, and collected folklore, they weave a tale and paint a picture with words that will keep that legacy from oblivion. We are pleased to present this collection, not only because it will bring a smile to each reader, but because it will play its part in this great effort to preserve the culture of the West.

Our hats are off to cowboys everywhere. We admire your lifestyle and your sense of humor—and we salute you.

—The Editors

Layle Bagley
Rexburg, Idaho

Born and raised on a ranch north of Rexburg, Idaho, Layle is president of the Cowboy Poets of Idaho. He is well known for his storytelling, outdoor cooking, and poetry, and says he gets most of his ideas from "stories, experiences, and mental ramblings." He loves the open spaces, animals, and freedom of the West.

POKEY

Now this is quite a story, and I guess it's based on fact.
About a guy named Pokey, who was usually off the track.

He was always full of ideas that took him quite astray.
When you got mixed up with Pokey, it didn't hurt to pray.

He wasn't much for schoolin', trouble was his favorite game.
Whenever things went cockeyed you could bet you'd hear his name.

One day his head got workin'; revenge was on his mind.
He'd had a run-in with his sister; he was plottin' things unkind.

He thought and thought about a lot of things that he could do.
It even worried him so hard, he 'bout swallowed all his chew.

The thought hit him when he spied it, that little house out back;
If he could catch her sittin' in it, he'd give her a real spat.

He worked and fixed and figured just what he'd planned to do.
He figured out a paddle that would swing up straight and true

And smack her on the bottom—that would be 'bout right.
It would put them even, but he knew he'd have a fight.

He pulled the rope to test it, and it worked out just fine.
The paddle really snapped on up—should leave a bright red line.

Patiently he waited for several hours or more.
He snoozed and dreamed of vengeance just to settle up the score.

And finally he saw it—the outhouse door was shut.
He had her at his mercy; he'd smarten up her butt.

He gave the rope a right smart yank and waited for the yell.
But everything was quiet, and he thought, "Now, what the hell?"

His work and careful planning just couldn't have gone wrong.
He should have heard some screamin' and cussin' going on.

He sneaked up very careful and barely looked around.
He expected a mad sister flying out with pants still down.

But no, all was quiet. He sneaked a peek inside.
What he saw caused a shiver to run up and down his hide.

He knew he was in trouble and could see nowhere to go.
He had made a fatal error that shook him to the soul.

Inside that smelly shanty, so rickety and rough,
Sat Pokey's stern old father, so big and mean and tough.

The paddle was well thought out and worked so very fine.
Old Pokey was in trouble, and red would be *his* behind.

The trick with wood and rope that he had thought so bold
Hit his old Dad in the privates and knocked him out plumb cold.

David J. Ball
Rigby, Idaho

Dave farms for a living and writes poetry as a hobby and a form of relaxation. Farming, he says, "brings a person in touch with the most important values in life—integrity, industry, honest dealings with people, hard work, and total enjoyment of one's surroundings." Poetry, he says, "is a way of expressing my thoughts and innermost feelings."

THE COWBOY AND THE GENIE

Ol' Sam'd had enough of the high plains cold,
So he went where travel tickets were sold.

Said he wanted to go where it's sunny and warm,
To see clouds floating by, not packing a storm.

An island vacation was bound to be his.
More fun than soda water plumb full of fizz.

His island he found, headed straight for the beach,
Where the cold couldn't come—he was way out of reach.

Living life on idle, no need for full throttle,
When surveyin' the beach he saw a fancy-style bottle.

He dallied up on that bottle, gave a yank on the cork,
Up popped a gal genie, prettier than all in New York!;

Said, "I've been stored in this bottle so long on the sand,
You are granted one wish that will be my command."

Well, this cowboy had a map of his old home range.
Upon this he would wish and would bring about change.

To his genie he said, "On this range live my pards.
I wish new trucks for all, and new Cads in their yards."

She told him no savvy, the request was too strange,
Another chance he was granted so his mind he could change.

So he wished for a lady who was truthful all the time,
Built hourglass style with honest heart and mind,

One that would snuggle, and sit upon his lap.
"HOLD ON," said the genie, "let's take another look at that map!"

Omar Barker
Rincon Montoso, New Mexico

Omar died in 1985, leaving behind over 2,000 poems and 1,500 short stories and novelettes. He was a writer, teacher, and legislator in New Mexico and received numerous honors and awards, including an induction into the Hall of Fame of Great Western Writers in the National Cowboy Hall of Fame.

BUCKAROO'S SQUELCH

Two buckaroos were rivals in the bronco-ridin' game:
Ol' Breezy's brag was wild and loud, ol' Rusty's mild and tame.
"There ain't no use in talkin', boys," ol' Breezy used to boast.
"I've won top ridin' money everywhere from coast to coast!
I've got ol' Rusty beat a mile at this here ridin' biz—
There ain't no use to argue, boys, for that's the way it is!"

Ol' Rusty never argued none, just rode 'em as they come,
A winnin' in some contests and a losin' out in some,
But never braggin' any on his ridin', even when
He scored up in the money over mighty salty men.

Then one time at a rodeo, the way it come about,
The finals lay between them two. There wasn't any doubt
But what whichever one of them scored high that final day
Would win the big first money. Well, ol' Breezy drew a bay
Whose daddy was a wildcat and whose mammy was a snake.
Ol' Breezy come out skiddin', and he couldn't find the brake!
One jump he lost a stirrup and the next he lost his hat.
That bronco sure did learn him to be an acrobat!

Ol' Breezy landed on his neck, he rode him on the rump,
But never hit the saddle more than every second jump.
The bronco didn't throw him off, but though the ride was funny,
It chalked him up "Disqualified"—and plumb outside the money.

Ol' Rusty drawed a snaky dun as bad as Breezy's bay,
But set the saddle snug and tight and rode him anyway.
That evenin' at the payoff, watchin' Rusty draw his cash,
Ol' Breezy kept on braggin' mighty free and mighty brash.
"You rode it lucky *this* time," he declared, "but just the same,
I'm forkeder than you are at this bronco-ridin' game!"

Ol' Rusty spoke up quiet like a heap of cowboys do,
And give his quiet answer to this braggin' buckaroo:
"Why, sure you are," he told him. "I agree with you, of course!
I only ride the saddle—*you* ride the whole danged horse!"

COWBOY AT COLLEGE
Omar Barker

I went up to a college, and they asked me what I knowed
To justify embarkin' on the education road.
I told 'em that my pa and ma had figgered I was smart,
For I could purt near always tell a horse and cow apart.
A cow's the one that wears the horns, a horse is what you ride,
And both of them most always wear the hairy part outside.

They asked me what I knowed about the history of the earth.
I told 'em that I understood it started at Fort Worth,
Where Adam, the first Texan, found a market for his steers,
And started raisin' buckaroos with red and hairy ears.
They asked about my algebra. I told 'em it was tough,
The way most any cowboy's gits who's ridden long enough.

They asked me what philosophy of life I favored most,
And that one sure did snub me right up to the snubbin' post.
I pondered some then told 'em that I always do my best
To aim my spittin' eastwards when the wind is in the west.
They asked about my grammar, and I told 'em she was dead.
They didn't mention Grandpa, but I told 'em what he'd said:
That any man was foolish and was surely bound to fail
Who'd kick a hog barefooted or twist a panther's tail.

I went up to this college, but I didn't stay there long,
For they asked a heap of questions, and my answers was all wrong.
At least that's how *they* figgered, like them college fellers do,
But I brought a prof back with me just to spend a week or two
A-ridin' on the rancho with a hoss between his knees,
Where the wolves are wild and curly, the coyotes all got fleas.

About this here professor I won't say no word unkind,
For he packs a heap of knowledge in that thing he calls his mind;
But now *my* lack of learnin' don't seem near so woebegone—
At least *I* know which end to put the horse's bridle on!

"PURT NEAR!"
Omar Barker

They called him "Purt Near Perkins," for unless the booger lied,
He'd purt near done most everything that he had ever tried.
He'd purt near been a preacher, and he'd purt near roped a bear;
He'd met up with Comanches once and purt near lost his hair.
He'd purt near wed an heiress who had money by the keg,
He'd purt near had the measles, and he'd purt near broke his leg.
He'd purt near been a trail boss, and accordin' to his claim,
He'd purt near shot Bill Hickok—which had purt near won
    him fame!
He'd purt near rode some broncs upon which no one else
    had stuck—
In fact he was the feller who had purt near drowned the duck!

Now mostly all the cowboys on the Lazy S B spread,
They took his talkin' with a grin and let him fight his head.
But one named Tom Maginnis sorter told it to him rough:
"You're ridin' with an outfit now where 'purt near' ain't enough!
We tie our lass ropes to the horn, an' what we ketch we hold,
And 'purt near' is one alibi we never do unfold!
In fact, right now I'll tell you that no word I ever hear
Sounds quite so plain damn useless as that little pair: 'purt near'!"
That's how ol' Tom Maginnis laid it out upon the line,
And like a heap of preachin' talk, it sounded mighty fine.
But one day Tom Maginnis, while a-ridin' off alone,
He lamed his horse and had to ketch some neighbor nester's roan
To ride back to the ranch on. But somewhere along the way
A bunch of nesters held him up, and there was hell to pay!
Tom claimed he hadn't stole the horse—just borrowed it to ride.
Them nesters hated cowboys, and they told him that he lied.
They cussed him for a horsethief and they'd caught him with
    the goods.

They set right out to hang him in a nearby patch of woods.
They had poor Tom surrounded, with their guns all fixed
to shoot.
It looked like this poor cowboy sure had heard his last owl hoot!
They tied a rope around his neck and throwed it o'er a limb,
And Tom Maginnis purt near knowed this was the last of him.
Then suddenly a shot rang out from somewhere up the hill!
Them nesters dropped the rope an' ran, like nesters
sometimes will
When bullets start to whizzin'. Tom's heart leapt up with hope
To see ol' Purt Near Perkins ridin' towards him at a lope.
"Looks like I purt near got here just in time," ol' Perkins said,
"To see them nesters hang you!" Tom's face got kinder red.

"You purt near did!" he purt near grinned. "They purt near had
me strung!
You're lookin' at a cowboy that has purt near just been hung!
And also one that's changed his mind—for no word ever said,
Can sound as sweet as 'purt near', when a man's been purt
near dead!"

THIRSTY COWBOY
Omar Barker

There's a sayin' out West, and it's true, I'll allow,
That a man who can't drink from the track of a cow
Ain't much of a cowboy; for where punchers ride,
There ain't babblin' brooklets on every side,
For a waddy to drink from when joggin' around.
He waters, like cattle, wherever it's found.
Sometimes there is gyp in the water he drinks;
Sometimes it is muddy, and sometimes it stinks.
Sometimes it's so thick where the cattle have pawed
That before it is swallered it has to be chawed.
But speakin' of water and cowpuncher thirst,
I'll tell you when cowpokes get thirsty the worst.
It's when, at a slow walk that's known as *andante*,
He's passin' in sight of some homesteader's shanty,
And yonder beneath a blue sunbonnet shows
The face of a nester gal hangin' out clothes.
Or maybe he glimpses her framed in the door,
Her yaller hair gleamin' like gold-bearin' ore,
And all of a sudden her face looks so pink,
His terrible thirst makes him stop for a drink.
He may have just drunk from a spring cold and clear
A half a mile back—and the drink he'll get here
May be tanky-warm; but the dipper it's in
Is handed to him by a gal with a grin

That's sure mighty friendly—though modest and shy.
So he drinks and he drinks like he sure 'nough was dry.
Then maybe he lingers a minute or two
And talks about horses, the way cowboys do,
Until, by the time he gets ready to leave,
She's noticed a button that's loose on his sleeve.
So she sews it back on. Well, that's how it goes
When cowboy sees nester gals hangin' out clothes!
For nothin' else makes him so thirsty for water
As a glimpse of a homesteader's pretty young daughter!

BEAR ROPIN' BUCKAROO
Omar Barker

Now ropin' bears (says Uncle Sid) is sure a heap of fun,
And a lot more gizzard thrillin' than to shoot 'em with a gun.
I roped a big ol' he one time when I was young and raw.
He must have weighed 500 pounds, and monstrous was his paw.

He'd wandered out upon the flats for cowchips, bugs, and such.
Them grubs and worms, they suit a bear like pretzels suit the Dutch.
I purt near didn't ketch him, for a bear can split the breeze,
And your pony's got to wiggle if he beats him to the trees.
But the roan that I was ridin', he was tough and mighty fleet.
He overhauled ol' bruin, and my loop was quick and neat.
It ketched him snug around the neck, and when he hit the end,
I heard the cinches stretchin', and I felt the saddle bend!
My pony put the brakes on 'til he sure 'nough plowed the ground.
It purt near made me sorry that there weren't no crowd around
To watch a salty hand like me demonsterate my skill
At learnin' Mister Bruin to obey my wish and will!

"Come on, ol' b'ar!" I bellered. "You're a wild and wooly scamp,
But I'm the apparatus that can lead you into camp!"
At first I feared the rope would bust. I'd lose him if it should.
About a minute later, boys, I wished to hell it would!
That bear r'ared up and popped his teeth—'twas like a
    pistol crack—
Then grabbed my rope, hand over hand, and come right up
    the slack.
I give a squall and swung my hat to slap him in the eyes,
But a he-bear ain't a critter that's easy to surprise.
My pony tried to quit me, but he had a bear in tow,
And a-clingin' to the saddle was a load he couldn't throw.
He got a-straddle of the rope, a log, a bush, a bear.

He wallered on his haunches, and he pawed the upper air.
Ol' bruin's jaws and paws and claws, they purt near had me skun.
My rope was anchored to the horn and wouldn't come undone.
Seemed like we fought for hours, and I couldn't see no hope,
When bruin bit my twine in two and quit us on the lope.

Now ropin' bears (says Uncle Sid) is sure a heap of fun.
At least I've heard folks claim it is—I never roped but one.
It ain't no special trick at all to snag one in your noose.
The ketch is mighty simple—*but it's hell to turn him loose!*

JUDGE BEAN'S BEAR
Omar Barker

Old-time trains on the S.P. Line,
Down where the sands of the Pecos shine,
Sometimes stopped at Vinegarroon
Where old Judge Bean had a quaint saloon
To which the passengers made a rush
To sample his famous "rub-o'-the-brush."
There, like as not, they'd pause to stare
Awhile at a big fat cinnamon bear
Chained to a post with the shade so scant
That the Texas sun made him puff and pant.

"That b'ar," ol' Judge Roy Bean would grin,
"Can do more tricks than a harlequin,
But he won't perform, the smart ol' skunk,
Till he's had some beer to make him drunk.
He talks like a human, cusses, too,
On about four quarts of good brown brew.
If any you gents would like to try it,
I've got the beer—if you want to buy it."

It never failed! Some traveling gent
With a wholesome hanker for merriment,
Across the Lone Star bar *kerplunk,*
Would pay for beer to get the bear drunk.
Four bits a bottle was Judge Bean's price.
The beer looked good, and it gurgled nice
As down the ol' bear's hatch it ran.
"He'll talk purty soon just like a man—
Just one more bottle will do the trick,"
Judge Bean would grin, "if he gits it quick!"

One more bottle . . . Alas! Too late!
The train would whistle! It wouldn't wait!
As travelers ran to resume their trip,
Judge Bean would pull at his whiskered lip:
"Bart, git that b'ar in outa the sun.
He's sold some beer. We've had some fun.
Give him some meat—he's earned a chunk.
Do you reckon he ever would git drunk?"

Virginia Bennett
Winthrop, Washington

Virginia was raised in an agricultural family in New Hampshire, but always "possessed a consuming passion for horses and things 'Western'." Eventually she moved out West and met her husband, Pete. Together, they've worked cow outfits all over the West for the last twenty-two years. Now their family manages a private guest ranch, and Virginia notes, "What I like best about ranching is the opportunity it affords families to work together. And I enjoy the brotherhood of cowboys."

NICE WORK IF YOU CAN GET IT

To: The Secretary of Agriculture up in Washington, D.C.
From: A guy who's been raisin' cattle since 1963.
Dear Sir: My friend, Buford Tully, from over by Kersey way,
Got a thousand-dollar check from the government today.

It was a payment for not raising hogs that he received—
The most money them hogs ever made him, I believe.
So, I'd like to go into the business . . . of not raising cows
And hope they pay as well as Buford's hypothetical sows.

In your expert opinion, which I know could never be wrong,
What is the best kind of ranch not to raise cows on?
Since I want to meet every letter of your governmental phrase . . .
What would be the best breed of cattle not to raise?

I'd rather not raise Brahmas; I can't stand that breed at all;
But if that's not the best breed not to raise, I won't raise
    Simmentals.
The hardest part of this program, as I understand,
Is keeping accurate records of the stock I don't have on hand.

If I get a thousand dollars for not raising fifty head,
Will I get twice that much for not raising a hundred instead?
I'm not going to raise four thousand cows, that way I'll start
    out small;
That'll net me eighty thousand dollars in no time at all.

Then I'll be able to afford not raising more cows next year,
And I'm considering the business of not raising exotic deer.
Since I won't be raising livestock, then my lifestyle will be
    cramped,
So I'll file for unemployment and I'll qualify for food stamps.

I never thought I'd admit it, but now I see that I've been wrong
And you bureaucrats have had the best idea all along.
Yep, your agricultural bail-out programs work as pretty as
    you please.
And would you let me know when you'll distribute more
    free cheese?

Storms on the Divide
Virginia Bennett

I saddled up a black Morgan mare,
Headed up through the timber to Cottonwood Crik;
She danced from the hint of a storm in the air,
But I figgered we'd get the job done quick.

And soon we'd be home, she in her stall;
We just needed to check on a few head.
So we inched down the rimrock and heard the stones fall
From her hooves down to the Jones' homestead.

As we walked past the cabin, I looked in the door;
There were the five girls in there, all bedded down.
Their calves were there, too, standin' on the dirt floor,
So I reined that black mare on around.

Those were the five I needed and I thought, "That's grand,"
To find 'em all right off the bat.
We'll just trot on home, then cover some land,
When a bolt of lightning hit to the right of my track.

The mare reared and jumped sideways; I almost fell,
But in time I gathered up all my reins
And grabbed for the horn and her mane, as well,
And felt the adrenaline rush through my veins.

The lightning sparked again, off to the other side,
Hittin' an old snag of a ponderosa tree.
The thunder crashed as only it does on the Divide.
The mare stood spraddle-legged, now, trustin' only me.

I shoulda gone back to that cabin and waited it out,
But I thought of my partner back at the camp,
And I knew he'd be worried and frantic with doubt;
I could just see him pacin' back and forth with the lamp.

So I whipped the mare, and she felt the spur,
And down through the valley we flew;
No time for a slicker, and the rain caused a blur
Of the awfullest lightnin' storm I ever knew.

It bounced off the ridges right above my face,
The electricity raised the hair on my neck;
The roar of the thunder urged on our race,
And the smell of sulphur made me sick.

I reined up in the trees, to let the mare blow,
And when she'd rested, across open fields we hurried.
I should've stayed holed-up in the timber, I know,
But I didn't want my partner to be worried.

I prayed to God to spare me; Lord, how it poured!
And soon I was lookin' down at our camp.
I waited in the trees 'til the lightnin' flashed once more,
Then made a dash toward that kerosene lamp.

First, I rubbed down the mare and put her in a stall,
Threw her a couple flakes of hay on the floor,
Then walked across the yard with my slicker as a shawl,
Crossed the cabin porch and flung open the door.

"You don't have to worry now, and look, I'm not bleeding,
But I've been through Hell; oh, good! You've got coffee on!"
But my husband looked up at me from the book he was reading
And blankly asked, "Oh, yeah? Were you gone?"

THE HAZARDS OF BRAGGIN'
Virginia Bennett

"I always have a walkin' horse,"
The cowboy said with pride.
"The one that's walkin' fastest
Is the only one I'll ride.

"And if I'm workin' with a colt
Who's a little lazy or slow,
I just whittle me a willow switch
And teach him how to go.

"There ain't a one that I can't train
To pick 'em up and put 'em down.
You'll recognize the ones I've broke;
They can really go to town.

"No, I've never failed to school one
To walk way ahead of his bit,
And if any horse is walkin' slower,
Then I ain't the one who's ridin' it."

Well, me and Gus and Bonnie
Rode along and let him have his say,
'Cause while the old feller was braggin',
He was openin' every gate that day!

Ed Brown
Merced, California

An elementary schoolteacher, Ed's ideas come from actual experience to outright theft. He has participated in many gatherings and has had poems published in three previous anthologies and in numerous magazines and newspapers. He doesn't know what he appreciates most about his lifestyle, as he's never lived anywhere but on a ranch.

BRONC RIDES

I know some boys can ride those broncs,
Allowin' no chance to throw 'em.
To tell about the tough ones I've rode
Would take half as long as this poem.

When I'm atop a buckin' horse
I cannot permit defeat,
So I stretch the reins, and choke the horn,
And spank 'em—with my seat.

Now horses must learn discipline,
And buckin' sure is wrong.
But I must be softhearted,
'Cuz I never spank 'em long.

COWBOYS' BOYS
Ed Brown

At every roping I've been to,
Should you agree or not,
The real competition's out there
In the parking lot.

The pint-sized and the peewees
All ignore the grandstand noise.
They've got a ten-steer of their own,
These kids, the cowboys' boys.

I've seen 'em rope a hay bale,
Or a dummy steer will do.
Then, of course, they'll rope each other
Or a local dog or two.

Twirling five-sixteenths with skill,
The action goes for hours.
The smallest kids get heeled and heeled,
Then turned out when they're soured.

Now the kid that I remember most
Could dang sure swing and toss it;
Ten for ten around the horns
Of this upright water faucet.

His loop was flat, and small, and quick.
He pulled his slack with skill.
A future wolf, both born and bred,
And waiting for the kill.

I told him, "Kid, yer ropin' tough
With that faucet for a dummy."
He just said, "Mister, ten bucks says
I can rope it when it's running."

MORE SHORTER
Ed Brown

I've got a friend and neighbor
Whose name is Kenny Wood.
We always help each other brand
And get along real good.

Eck Safford was Ken's uncle,
Who ran the Howard Ranch.
He'd help his neighbors brand their calves
Each time he had the chance.

And they'd return the favor
To brand the Howard calves,
The kind of neighbor trading
Good cowmen like to have.

One time he helped a neighbor
And pitched in like he should.
This feller hadn't been here long,
Spoke English "no too good."

So Uncle Eck, he got the job
Of marking the calves' ears,
Which he took on like all he did,
With experience of years.

Now the earmark of this feller, Joe,
Was a single crop on the left.
Eck Safford had a fair idea,
So he just kind of guessed . . .

That an inch off the tip was ample,
Just custom-made to order,
But Joe spoke out as the calf got up,
"Now cut that ear more shorter."

So the next one that the boys dragged out,
He sliced off a fraction more.
Old Joe barked out, "More shorter," again
And acted a little bit sore.

Now Eck sure wanted to do right,
So on the very next calf,
He took this greenie at his word
And cut that ear in half.

At this old Joe got plumb upset;
We recall his words today,
When he bellered out for all to hear
"More shorter THE OTHER WAY!"

Bruce Caswell
Enumclaw, Washington

B ruce is a blacksmith and lives in the foothills of the
Cascade Mountains of Washington. About his lifestyle
he says, "Except for a few modern conveniences,
ranching is still pretty much the same as it was a hundred
years ago. I like the fact that I use the same methods when
working with horses that old-time cowboys used." Some of the
inspiration for his poetry comes from stories passed down by
old-timers, and stories that he's read about the Old West.

RANCHER'S REWARD

An old rancher died and left behind
his wife of forty years;
she missed him so, but don't you know,
she dried up all her tears

When she heard of an Indian woman
who could talk to the other side;
now she never had really believed in that stuff,
but she figured she'd give it a try.

So she went to see the woman,
and prayin' it weren't no prank,
she asked the woman to put her in touch
with her dear departed Frank.

Well, the woman started chanting,
and soon a voice rang clear,
"Who in the hell's disturbin' my work?"
"It's me, Frank, it's Marion; I'm here!"

"Why, Marion, how are you doin'?"
"Oh, not bad for a grieving wife;
I just wanted to see how you're gettin' along,
there in the afterlife."

"Well, truthfully, it couldn't be any better.
There's blue sky as far as you can see,
and big puffy clouds floatin' over my head,
and grass clear up past my knees.

"And there's cows, hundreds of beautiful cows.
They're grazing all over the place.
Why, I ain't done nothin' since I got here
'cept walk around with a smile on my face!"

She said, "Well, it's good to know that you're happy,
and I'm glad I got to talk to you.
And it's nice to know that heaven has a ranch,
so you'll always have somethin' to do."

"Oh, I've got plenty to keep me busy;
why, each day I meet my quota.
But Marion, dear, I ain't up in heaven;
I'm a bull out in South Dakota!"

BRAIN TRANSPLANT
Bruce Caswell

One day this rancher got throw'd from his hoss,
and took one hell of a thump to the head.
The doctor told his family that without a brain transplant,
in a week to ten days he'd be dead.

"Now, we're a family of limited means,
but the savings account we will drain.
We've never had to buy this kind of thing before;
what's the goin' price on a secondhand brain?"

He said, "For ten thousand dollars I can get you a lawyer's brain
that belonged to this feller named Brown.
That's a pretty good price for an attorney's brain;
he was one of the slickest lawyers around!

"Twenty thousand dollars will get you a doctor's brain—
a research specialist from UCLA.
With this kind of brain your daddy could do nothin'
but set and ponder all day.

"I've got one other brain that I know he would like,
but the price might be a little bit high.
It's a bull rider's brain, and it costs fifty thousand dollars.
But they say he was a hell-of-a nice guy!"

Well, they knew which brain their daddy would want,
but they just didn't have that much bread.
So they talked it over and finally decided
they'd take the doctor's brain instead.

But why would a bull rider's brain cost so much?
This issue still had 'em confused.
The doctor said, "Well, it's simple; you see,
that brain's like new; it's never been used!"

Wayne Cornett
Midland, Texas

Wayne is president of the Texas Cowboy Poet's Association and has participated in several poetry gatherings. He says his ideas for his poetry come from "day-to-day experiences and remembering incidents from my past." He is retired from a gas utility company and helps work cattle on a friend's ranch.

THE TALL TIMID COWBOY

A West Texas girl married a tall timid cowboy.
This lanky cowpuncher stood six feet six.
It didn't take her long 'til she discovered
That her sleepin' was in a terrible kinda fix.

This ole boy was so long when he laid on the bed,
He reached from corner to diagonal corner.
This poor girl had to curl up in a little ball.
That was one thing that he failed to warn her.

In just over a year their first baby came.
Now she found that she needed a nursing bra.
She asked him to go in the store and buy it.
That timid cowboy just blushed and said, "Nah!"

He went in the store, wearing a sheepish grin.
He said, "I came in here to buy things for my wife."
But he was too timid to ask the lady clerk for a bra.
So he said, "I'll just take that pocketknife."

Knife in pocket, he stood around on the sidewalk.
Then he sauntered to the truck across the street.
He said, "I just couldn't ask her for that bra.
Why, just look at me, I'm as red as a fresh beet."

She replied, "I wish you weren't always so timid.
That clerk is accustomed to waiting on such men."
So he psyched himself up, he got out of the truck, and
This timid cowboy went back to the store again.

Back inside he found he was in the music department.
He thought, "I've just got to buy my wife's things."
The same lady clerk asked, "Sir, may I help you?"
"Well, uh, yes, ma'am, I'll take these fiddle strings."

He was in a quandary to face the clerk or his wife.
Here this ole boy stood caught in the middle.
"Ma'am, I sure do need your help." "Certainly sir,
First tell me, is she gonna whittle or fiddle?"

"Ma'am, clerk, lady, I know that you have a job to do.
But for me, doin' this just isn't very much fun.
To answer your question about whittle or fiddle:
By doggies, she's not going to do either one.

"Asking this is mighty hard, 'cause I'm a cowman,"
While he was twistin' on his cuffs till he tore-um.
"You see, what I really need, ma'am, is a nursing bra."
She replied, "I didn't know cows ever wore-um."

He was trembling all over when she asked, "What size?"
If he couldn't tell her, he knew she would laugh.
So recollecting and now judging by his hat,
He answered, "Give me a seven and a half."

Bob Court
Issaquah, Washington

ob has a small spread near the Cascade Mountains where he raises Appaloosa quarter horses. He also teaches western history to high schoolers nearby. Of his lifestyle, he says, "I've always believed that 'cowboy' was more than the hat and horse. It's a spirit, a way of thinking about things. It's taking care of the land and the animals that live on it with dignity." Bob notes that a pair of spurs have hung on his door for as long as he can remember . . . and he expects they always will.

ROPIN' THE IRON HORSE

Mad Dog Bill McCorkle
was the greatest roper I ever saw.
With a forty-foot line he could lay it out fine
over horns or hoof or paw.

I seen him catch mustangs, bulls and calves,
even coyotes and bears for fun.
But once drunk as a skunk I watched him debunk
every ropin' legend under the sun.

On the way back from Laredo, headin' to Cotulla,
we'd drunk up the saloon in that town.
Dizzy with whiskey I was feelin' right tipsy
and felt the ground turnin' 'round.

I said, "I had too much, Bill, for I'm sensin' a tremblin'
'neath the hooves of this horse of mine."
He said, "Don't worry, Bud, or swaller yer cud,
it's just a train rumblin' hard down the line."

And sure as a mosshorn will lay down in a wallow,
a locomotive puffed over the hill.
And as I looked to my side I got quite a surprise,
for a weird look come over Ol' Bill.

He says, "I roped every critter from the Rio to the Powder,
and you know I'm the best, of course.
I've even set my riata on lizards and rattlers,
now I'll hang a loop on that there iron horse!

"I'll bet you my saddle, my horse and my gun,
and will throw in a Confederate dollar bill,
that I can hog-tie that critter in top cowhand time
after bringin' it to a standstill."

I reached for his reins but he set spur a-howlin'
and took off toward that train at a lope.
Then he kicked in with a burst and I expected the worst
as he formed up a loop in his rope.

I followed at a gallop but Bill had pulled up
alongside that engine on its track.
And I heard him yell, "Yaaaaaa!" as he threw his line true
and the rope tightened 'round its black stack.

"Hellfire!" I says as my mind become sober
and Mad Dog goes to dally the horn,
but the Lord was a-watchin' and afore he could do so,
the slack left and Bill was airborne!

The next thing I saw was him settin' his feet
like a bulldogger out of the chute.
He disappeared in the dust but I knew he was afoot
for the sparks were still flyin' off his boots.

I rode by the train, jumped on aboard
and grabbed that startled engineer by the collar.
But it was so loud he didn't stop the engine
for I reckon he couldn't hear me holler.

So I pulls out my Colt and sticks it up in his nose,
though I suppose it really wasn't his fault.
But he picked up my meanin', pulled back on the throttle
and brought that iron horse to a halt.

I looked over the side and there was Mad Dog Bill
with his body a-covered in soil.
His shirt was ripped off and his boots were on fire,
but he calmly put his rope back in coils.

"You win the bet, Bud, though I roped him clean
and dragged him to a halt, you know.
But I lost my 'piggin' string and I can't snug him down,
so I reckon I'll just have to let 'im go."

Elizabeth Ebert
Lemmon, South Dakota

Elizabeth and her husband, S. J., are retired ranchers who still live on the same place they bought when they were married forty-eight years ago. Their son runs the operation now while they spend a lot of time traveling (often to cowboy poetry gatherings). Elizabeth has three books published and has been included in three anthologies. She says, "What I like best about ranch life is the feeling of being close to the land. I like the quiet and the solitude . . ."

THE CEMETERY

We have a small town cemetery
    On a little hill out on the prairie,
And all our folks are buried there,
    But there's no such thing as perpetual care.
So we go out there every spring
    To mow and rake and do the things
That someone always has to do,
    And all our neighbors work there, too.

Last spring the graves were a disgrace,
    For cactus had overrun the place
And was choking out the prairie grasses
    In ugly, prickly, spiny masses.
So a group of us decided that we
    Would all get together one day and see
If with spades and shovels and muscles stout
    We could dig those pesky critters out.

When I told my husband of our plan,
   (Now remember, he's kind of deaf) and Man!
He jumped from his chair and he stomped around
   And he ranted and raved 'til I finally found
What his temper tantrum was all about—
   He thought we were digging the CATHOLICS out!

THE LAST GREAT RABBIT HUNT
Elizabeth Ebert

Back when we first were married we were short of cash, and so
We decided to hunt rabbits, just to make some extra dough.
Old Sure-Shot with his twenty-two, and me the True Believer,
Content to tag along behind and act as his retriever.

Those old jacks sure were plentiful, we really were in luck,
For every four we took to town would bring about a buck.
But we'd not stoop to sell that way; we thought it would be nifty
To wait to take them 'til we had some forty-five or fifty.

Then we'd have a celebration, take in a show, no doubt,
A glass of wine, or maybe two, and we'd have supper out.
So we hunted through the winter every chance we got,
For back there in the forties a dollar meant a lot.

We piled those rabbits on the roof on the north side of a shed,
And the last time that we tallied we had a hundred head.
And then the blizzards hit us, and the wind it never stopped.
We shoveled snow, and broke the ice, and pitched hay 'til
    we dropped.

And just as sudden came the sun and a warm and gentle breeze;
We calved those doggone heifers out in mud up to our knees.
And on that wind was wafted such a stench across the lot
That, finally, we remembered those rabbits we'd forgot.

I said, "Today you'll have to haul your rabbits out of here."
His most ungallant answer was, "Those are OUR rabbits, dear!"
And so we made a compromise, and I, with much foreboding,
Said I would load the rabbits up if he'd do the unloading.

I shinnied up onto the roof of that evil-smelling shed
And held my breath and shoveled off those hundred stinking dead.
And then we took off for the hills far from our small abode,
So he could fill his bargain's part and empty out the load.

I sat there in the pickup, content I'd done my share,
But minute followed minute and the rabbits still were there.
I couldn't see him anyplace 'til I followed up a hunch;
There, on the ground, my husband lay a-chucking up his lunch.

Was this the macho hero that I'd tried so hard to win?
This sorry, sniveling sissy with the vomit on his chin?
Great was my disillusionment, I'd really had enough!
I'd show what I was made of! I'd prove that I was tough!

I jumped into that pickup box and grabbed up one big jack
And fueled by righteous anger I hurled it out the back.
But at that very moment, above the truck's tailgate,
Appeared the sickly visage of my wretched, retching mate.

I swear I tried to stay that throw; I really tried my best.
But that rank and rotten rabbit hit him squarely in the chest!
I told him I was sorry, and I tried hard not to laugh,
For the situation's humor somehow missed my better half.

Full forty years have passed and still these memories make
    us wince.
Let's close the book. Suffice to say we've shot no rabbits since!

Fred G. Ellis
Silt, Colorado

Fred had a dream of being a cowboy when he was a kid, and did not see that dream come true until he was over forty. Now he performs a one-man cowboy poet show, manages a ranch in Meeker, Colorado, and says, "Never give up a dream. I believe God gives them to us to pursue." Fred feels that the freedom of the ranching life "lets you think about God's creation, life's problems, and how they . . . can all fit together for the good of mankind."

DEAR MR. FOREMAN

Dear Mr. Foreman,

I told you I was from the city the day that I was hired,
So why in only three short days this note that I am fired?
Something must have gone astray as your temper blew.
Oh, please give me one more chance to make a buckaroo.

I bought a big hat, red bandana and a leather vest,
Soon I'll have the boots, chaps, spurs and all the rest.
I will learn the famous cowboy grin and talk the cowboy talk.
A cob between my cheeks I'll place to master the cowboy walk.

I'm sorry for committing a horrible greenhorn sin;
Rest assured you'll never see me milk your bull again.
The next time that I saddle—I know that I will pass;
The saddle horn will not be faced toward the horse's tail.

Let us start anew; all the damage has been done.
Besides, it wasn't all my fault I branded your left bun.
I have promised all the hands, if I ever chew again,
Before I spit I'll look around and check prevailing wind.

This is all I've ever wanted; to cowboy I have yearned.
I beg you, Sir, let me stay, my lessons I have learned.
Keep me on; don't ship me off like some steer to the slaughter,
For if you do, I promise you, I'll come back and marry your daughter.

DEAR MR. AUCTIONEER
Fred G. Ellis

Dear Mr. Auctioneer,

I was at the auction Saturday past
And I think ya gaveled a little too fast.

I moved my hand to shoo flies away;
You said, "Sold!" an' I bought a bay.

I waved to a friend a few rows down;
Bought ten hogs that was walkin' 'round.

I went to give my nose a wipe;
You gave your gavel an awful swipe.

They yelled my number an' what did I see
But a big Brahma bull lookin' right back at me.

I don't like to complain an' I hates to be kickin's,
But what do I do with ten thousand chickens?

Donna Hacking Erickson
Rexburg, Idaho

When Donna was young she picked up potatoes to earn
the money to buy her first Hereford heifer, which then
had a heifer calf, and Donna was in business. She is
now a homemaker and mother of eleven children. Of the
ranching lifestyle, she loves most the good down-to-earth
people, the horses, and the closeness to nature. The
inspiration for this poem came from a story passed down to
Donna from her grandmother.

THE ODOR AT THE RIDDLE RANCH DANCE

The month was June and the rising moon
Was encouragin' thoughts of romance,
When that handsome Slim, with a fetchin' grin,
Asked blonde-haired Maybelle to dance.

She sweetly answered, "Why, I'd be pleasured,"
So he tucked her hand in his arm.
He walked like a king, and she like his queen,
Onto the floor of the barn.

But then she sniffed and looked quite miffed.
She sniffed, and sniffed again.
She shook her head, glared Slim dead,
Then left like a huffy hen.

Slim's hopes were dashed; he felt right bashed.
He scratched his head perplexed.
"Boss," said he, "how can this be?
Her leavin' has me vexed."

Boss wrinkled his nose, rose up on his toes.
"Slim," he said, "take off your sox."
So out went Slim where the lights were dim
To avoid the women's gawks.

He came back in and asked Jennie Lynn
If she would be his partner.
She smiled right nice as she looked in his eyes,
But then one whiff disheartened her.

She leaned somewhat close, got a pungent dose.
Her face turned a sickly green.
She was durn near death when she took a breath.
"You should be in quarantine!"

"Well now, Slim," Boss said with a grin,
"Did you throw those sox away?"
"Of course not, Boss. They're good for one wash.
They're in my pocket for another day."

Florene Flatt
Lubbock, Texas

Florene and her husband began ranching in Paris, Texas, in 1982 and quickly found that they were "cowboys at heart." She has participated in cowboy gatherings in Texas and New Mexico and says that "an emotion that is expressed in a poem is better than petals pressed in a book. Words you can keep in your heart."

LAST LAUGH

Bill said to Joe, "I need a place
to put this scrawny little bull."
Joe said to Bill, "Bring him over;
I've grass to keep him and mine all full.

"If it won't make him feel too bad
to hang around my registered stuff,
My Big Red will push him around
and maybe he'll get tough."

Each morning as they drank their coffee,
Joe and the Missus laughed to see
That little black bull leaning on the fence
as tired as he could be.

They said, "He ain't got the energy
to put one foot in front of the other,
He must have had a sorry dad
and an even sorrier mother."

The weeks went by and Bill pulled in
and loaded up his prize.
Joe and the Missus laughed as they left
till the tears ran from their eyes.

Joe said, "I wonder if Bill will use him
to sire and get a blue-ribbon herd;
The buyers will come from far and near
whenever they get the word."

The months went by and Joe was due
a beautiful registered crop;
The time was here, and any day
the calves would begin to drop.

One came, then two, and three and four
and so on to number twenty.
The calves were coming fast and easy;
the numbers they were plenty.

But what made Joe's face so sad and long
and the Missus' jaw so slack
Was every durn one of them calves that dropped
was gangly, skinny, and BLACK!

Lloyd M. Gerber
Eagle, Idaho

L loyd grew up on the Rock Creek Ranch in Utah, accessible only by a two-day pack trip, where his family raised sheep and cattle. He has been a lawyer, teacher, manager, CEO, and cowboy poet—as well as a guest on the *Tonight Show* with Johnny Carson in 1989.

REAL OR FAKE

There are fewer cowboys on the ranch
    Than used to be, that's true,
But in the cities they're as thick as flies,
    And I don't mean just a few.

The city pokes can't ride a horse
    Or rope a cow or steer,
But they dress up like the real thing
    When they go to drink their beer.

I see them in ten-gallon hats
    Of different kinds and makes.
Some are on real cowpokes' heads,
    Others sit on fakes.

So how do you know the real
    When they look the same that way?
I can tell you how to tell,
    And it won't matter what they say.

'Tain't the spangles, sports, and doodads
    Hung on collar, front, and cuff.
'Tain't the gaudy-colored kerchiefs,
    Or any of that stuff.

'Tain't those big belt buckles
    That make their trousers sag.
'Tain't the shirts that look like doilies,
    Of which they like to brag.

'Tain't their Liberace belts that
    Go twining 'round their girth.
'Tain't anything that glitters
    That makes up a cowpoke's worth.

No, the test is not the clothes he wears;
    For that he gives no hoot.
The test that proves a cowpoke true
    Is—manure on his boot.

THOSE CATS
Lloyd M. Gerber

It happened on Range Valley Mountain,
 Our summer ground, you know:
One day's trip with one lone pack,
 Not very much to show.

Now I should have known better
 Than to do what I did;
I should have been smarter,
 But I acted like a kid.

"We'll pack that little black gelding;
 Won't be much of a load.
He's never had a saddle on,
 But it will help him 'til he's rode.

"We'd better throw on some beans and stuff,
 And poison for those rats.
There'll be plenty of room, of course,
 So throw on those three cats.

"Just tighten the straps on the panniers
 So the cats can get some air.
We wouldn't want them dyin'
 While we're packin' 'em over there."

So we packed the little black gelding
 With food and other stuff I said,
Then headed for Van Duzan Ridge
 Without a worry or dread.

The black was spooked and skittish
    As we headed up the trail,
And I wondered then what he would do
    If the lid on the cats should fail.

We'd been gone about ten minutes
    When those cats began to yell,
And the little black kept looking back
    A-wondering, what the _____!

Well, it wasn't very much farther
    'Til one cat on the top did ride.
That left only two of them,
    Fighting it out inside.

Suddenly I got smart;
    I knew there would be trouble.
I said, "I'll get those cats repacked;
    I'll do it on the double."

But when I tried to stop the horse,
    He just started making time
And dodged past my outstretched rope
    By turning on a dime.

I couldn't stop the horse
    So I could fix the things;
THREE cats now were perched on top;
    That horse would soon take wings.

The cats were getting skittish,
    Like they knew not what to do.
The black kept going faster
    And was getting skittish, too.

One cat drifted towards his tail;
    The gelding took a jump.
Down he came with all three cats
    A-clingin' to his rump.

He went a-bucking through the trees,
    A-goin' like a shot.
The cats with talons sunk clear in
    Were hanging where they caught.

We barely got a glimpse of him
    As he dodged both here and there;
But once we saw a cat go
    A-flying through the air.

When we finally caught him,
    His coat was flecked in white.
Panniers, pads, food and cats
    Were thrown off in his flight.

We gathered it up in bits and pieces,
    Covering a mile or more;
And we tied it right back on him,
    Though we were a bit more poor.

For though we found the beans and stuff
    And poison for the rats,
We never did find hide nor hair
    Of any of those cats.

Peggy Godfrey
Moffat, Colorado

Peggy has been ranching for a living for twenty-one years and loves everything about the ranching lifestyle— "working with animals, solitude, scenery, the earth and water on my hands, in my boots, up my nose, etc." Her poems, which have been heard at many poetry gatherings, are often drawn from actual experiences first told as stories.

GET IT RIGHT, FELLA!

The local radio stock report
 that happens at ten 'til eight
Proceeds in routine manner
 while I sop eggs off my plate.
One morning a fill-in announcer
 was doing the morning news,
Reporting prices on cattle and hogs,
 bucks and lambs and ewes.
He wallowed in this strange set of wordage
 (oh, how a paycheck is earned);
Out o'er the airwaves for valley ranchers,
 his stock report crashed and burned.
Now I can see a fella call
 a baby lamb a peewee,
But Heaven knows, when they grow,
 we call 'em ewes, not eewees!

SELLIN' POSTHOLES
Peggy Godfrey

On a lazy after-dinner
We were all too full to move;
Conversation drifted aimlessly
Through the economic grooves.

Robert was a moanin',
Quite sure he'd be unpaid
For 300 feet of dry well
And casin' he had laid.

Us ranchers bemoaned the weather
An' the dropped-out price of cattle;
Seems the harder you try to win,
The quicker you lose the battle.

We joked 'bout pullin' that dry well
And tryin' to make it pay
By plantin' the sucker somewhere else—
Sure, we could find a way.

The others at the table
Were glassy-eyed and dull—
The thing that often happens
After supper when you're full.

But spurred by our ambition,
We other three made way
To study all the options
To make that dry well pay.

Let's pull that well right outa there
An' lay it on the ground.
We'll cut to fit the loggin' truck.
How does that plan sound?

We'd sell the stuff for postholes,
Make it clear when we got paid
These holes are drilled by factory—
Not crooked, rough, handmade.

We had no plans to fool a soul;
A hole is what we're sellin'—
Just turnin' lemons to lemonade,
Not tryin' to make a killin'.

We discussed our reputation
And decided we could spare
An extra foot in twenty
In case they weren't cut square.

As for storage, we can set 'em
Almost anyplace:
Stock can get around 'em;
They don't take too much space.

The 10- and 12-inch holes we'd sell
As four-foot corner stock.
The 6 and 8 we'd sell by 3s
To plant in clay or rock.

We was feelin' mighty proud
Of money almost made
For savin' Robert's drillin' rig
With cash that he'd get paid.

This after-dinner fantasy
Was wearin' mighty thin
When, from outside our threesome,
Another voice wedged in:

"Ya got no tool to drive 'em.
How will you keep 'em straight?
An' how ya gonna count 'em?
You'll lose at any rate.

"No chain will hold and off they'll roll.
You guys are gonna look funny.
I doubt you'll ever sell a load.
Don't count on makin' money."

We looked at one another,
Our smugness was not hid.
She said we'd never sell a load—
We figured we just did.

Jim Green
Fort Smith, Northwest Territory, Canada

J im was raised next to the mountains in the ranching country of southwest Alberta. Besides his writing, he does some guiding and outfitting to fill in the lean times. "After 30 years wrangling most any kind of job a man can lay his hands to, I'm finally writing full time and eating fairly regular—almost." He also travels around telling tales as well as writing and recording a radio series of old-time stories.

JUGHANDLE SMITH GOES TO TOWN

It usually wouldn't make no nevermind
one way or the other. Jughandle would
have himself a big time on Saturday,
often heading home dead to the world,
but his team knew where the barn was.

That day some idiot closed a road gate
so when Dad 'n' Uncle Zeke happened by
there was the team stopped at the wire,
Jughandle pounding his ear, so naturally
Dad 'n' Zeke unhitched 'n' hid the horses.

By 'n' by Jug stirred 'n' opened one eye.
"Am I Yughandle Smith or ain't I?" sez
he. "If I am, I've lost my team again
and if my name ain't Yughandle Smith,
by the Yesus, I found myself a buggy."

NO TIME IN SWEETGRASS
Jim Green

Wheeling south across the line
to the Sweetgrass Sunday rodeo
gunna cheer ole Kenny Luther on
when he rides them crooked horn
bulls and outlaw bareback broncs.
Daryl hucks the cap in the ditch
as we blast on outta Lethbridge
so it's Orange Crush and vodka
clear to the Montana border
and then some grandstand beer
in this Sunday rodeo town.

Cowboys and cayuses and busted
gear flying around in the dust
when the announcer grumbles
Luther's only got five minutes
to claim his riding stock
or they're gunna turn it out.
But Daryl ain't having none
of that shit   no sir
Kenny ain't showed up   so
drunk as he is   Daryl starts
climbing them wooden steps
to sign the stock in his name.

But stairs can be kinda tricky
you gotta figure'm out just right
with a landing about halfway.
So it's up this way for a while
around the edge of the landing
then double back the other way

for the last hike to the top
which Daryl manages to navigate
slow   and none too steady
but somehow   he makes it
until   with one step left
he hesitates   grabs for the rail
and Daryl loses it.

Daryl's turned loose his own self
flying arse over teakettle
a-pinwheeling bassackwards
boots and elbows flailing
the dust-choked sky
down them wooden rodeo stairs
his mind screaming   "TOO SOON
NOT YET   I WASN'T SET"
his voice exploding in his ears
"CLOSE THAT GODDAMN GATE."

But it's too late for Daryl
somersaulting outtacontrol backwards
down the judging-stand stairs
crashing into the landing
smashing through the 2 x 4 rails
taking to the open air
dropping six slow feet
to land   WHUMP   in a limp heap.
A puff of dust whoofs up.

And here's this seasoned judge
peering down over the railing
watching this amazing spectacle
of pure balance and poise
leans into the microphone
and he announces   "NO TIME
NO TIME FOR THAT COWBOY."
Daryl scrambles to his feet
don't wanna get trampled
by no haywire rodeo horse
and the crazy crowd roars.
Daryl scoops up his old hat
clamps it sidewise on his head
and by God he bows to the folks.
Damned if they don't cheer again
so the judge   he beams real big
like it was all his idea
leans into that mike again
"NO TIME
give him a good hand folks
that's all he's taking home today."

Carol Hample
Bozeman, Montana

Carol makes her living as a CPA in public practice. She has published a book of poetry, read at poetry gatherings, and received the first Golden Star Award for Poetry from the *Montana Poet* magazine. She lives in Bozeman, where she enjoys the "clear air, long views for stretching the eyeballs, and the rugged beauty all around."

THE STEERING WHEEL

I was often in trouble and never got bored
In the days I was driving my Model T Ford.
It was simple to operate, easy to fix,
If you knew how it worked and a couple of tricks.

It had brakes and reverse and a low and high gear,
But you had to push hard with your foot, that was clear.
And the steering wheel I had replaced on my T,
For the Model A version was larger, you see.

It was thicker though, too, with no room for the nut,
But if there was a problem, I didn't know what.
It was keyed so the wheel wouldn't slip, anyway,
And the steering was easy. I liked it that way.

My friend Johnny and I often worked as a team.
If we didn't have chores, we would cook up some scheme.
We were hauling a barrel of water one day
Up a pretty steep hill for the T, I would say.

Now the barrel was topless, so Johnny was riding
In back to prevent that old barrel from sliding.
The steep part was rocky, the going was rough,
But we're under control, and it wasn't so tough.

I push hard on the pedal to keep it in gear,
And to brace I pull up on the wheel as I steer.
Well, it came off and hit me smack dab on the nose,
But that smacking was only the start of my woes.

Well, I had to grab something to keep pushing down,
For the brakes wouldn't hold, though I felt like a clown.
With one hand on the throttle and one holding on,
I can't wipe my face, and my dignity's gone,

With the blood and the tears I can't see and can't steer
And can't stop on that slope—oh, my plight was severe!
And poor Johnny in back as we jerked up the hill
Was still holding the barrel so it wouldn't spill.

After lurching and jerking our way to the top,
Where the brakes finally held and we came to a stop,
We were under control and were glad we had fought 'er,
But had to go back down the hill for more water.

Joel Hayes
Douglasville, Georgia

Joel is a lineman for a telephone company and also raises "paint horses, goats, and a lot of times, eyebrows." He has been to several poetry gatherings and says he and his partner introduced cowboy poetry to the Southeast. He notes that as "a cowboy living in Georgia, people sometimes don't know how to take me."

FULL VALUE

Rip, he was a cowboy,
as good a one as I have known.
He knew about handling cattle
and how a hoolihan was thrown.

He could double hock a calf
and ease it to the ground—
Have it to the branding fire
before it knew he was around.

But he was careful with his money;
unusual for his breed.
He'd never spend a penny
unless there was desperate need.

Rip, he was a chewer,
though he griped about the price.
Just to get his money's worth
he chewed his tobacco twice.

We were in town on payday
and Rip, he shocked us all.
Bought two state lotto tickets
down at the old pool hall.

We kidded him 'bout being wasteful—
just throwing his money away.
Blowing two whole dollars gambling
on a puncher's meager pay.

In the paper some weeks later,
Rip's number did appear.
He was the grand-prize winner;
he was grinning from ear to ear.

The pot was fifteen million bucks;
He began to hoot and holler.
Then it struck him dead to right—
He'd plumb wasted that other dollar.

COMPUTER RANCHING
Joel Hayes

I had six hundred mama cows.
　　I knew them all by sight.
I could usually spot a problem
　　If one wasn't acting right.

Then we got a brand new owner—
　　He's a new-age cattleman.
Said, "Sell the horses. Buy computers."
　　That's his profit-making plan.

"We'll put each cow on computer.
　　She'll be on a floppy disk.
There'll be no need to ride the pasture,
　　She'll be right there on the list.

"We will have better records,
　　Printouts available to all.
Calf weights will be higher
　　When we ship them in the fall.

"Yes, the computer is the answer
　　To the modern rancher's plight.
The labor will be so easy,
　　We won't be tired at night."

So I asked, "With this computer
　　Will I get a cut in pay?
How is it at building fences,
　　Spreading salt, and hauling hay?

"Will this computer know the difference
    'Tween a heifer and a steer?
Can it scatter the bulls just right
    So the cows will calve next year?"

The boss said, "Trust in the computer,
    It will never let you down!"
So I rode a CR TV screen,
    And the boss, he went to town.

Yeah, I punched cows from a computer,
    And the boss was surely right.
There ain't much work to do now,
    'Cause the last cow died last night.

Charlie Hunt
Rapid City, South Dakota

Charlie formerly "cowboyed, rodeoed and ranched" and is now a freelance writer, minister, and real estate appraiser. His book, *For Cowboys, Campers, an' Common Folk, If You Ain't One of These, Don't Buy It*, is in its second printing. Many of his ideas for poems come from trail drives, memories, or working cattle and horses.

THE RASCAL

The bulls gathered off in the corner
    Were spinnin' a yarn or two.
The Gelbvieh bragged on the calves he had sired—
    Their size—an' their numbers, too.

The Charolais then told of his prowess
    An' topped the Gelbvieh, of course,
But the Simmental quickly put them both down
    As he bragged without any remorse.

The other bulls kept up their braggin'
    But the Angus bull said not a word.
He jist quietly slipped out to the pasture
    And joyfully bred the whole herd.

Tony Ilardi
Truckee, California

Tony is currently a business office manager for a power company, but he has been performing cowboy poetry and music since he was three. He grew up in the Truckee area, where his family has resided since 1871 and where his grandfather was the town blacksmith. Tony started working on cattle and sheep ranches when he was a kid and enjoys "the animals, the ranching people and way of life. The ranchers and farmers are 'salt of the earth' folks."

OLD JOKER

The winter sure gets long
in a line shack by yourself.
By January, you've read up
every book upon the shelf.

And you long for a companion
to help you while the hours away,
just to visit or play cards,
to help you end your day.

Old Pete he was determined
that he'd not be bored this year.
He said he had a surefire plan
and I'd be the first to hear.

He said, "I bought a real smart dog
and I named the critter Joker.
I'll have lots of time this winter
to teach him a little poker."

Well, I thought that he was joking
and I teased old Pete that day,
but he was downright serious,
and this is what he had to say.

"You know I'm good with animals;
I can teach them anything.
Why, I even had a parrot once
and I taught that bird to sing.

"Just give me until January,
and you'll get a big surprise,
'cause you'll see a dog play poker
right before your very eyes."

It was New Year's Day in '88
when I rode to see ol' Pete.
He sure seemed glad to see me;
he said it was a treat.

I informed him that I came
to play a little poker.
Told him I could hardly wait
to play some hands with Joker.

Well, the three of us sat down,
and Pete he dealt a hand.
To my surprise the dog knew
when to fold and when to stand.

I said, "Pete, my hat's off to you.
Ol' Joker, he plays real good!"
But Pete said, "The dog just doesn't play
as well as I thought he would.

"He's got some real good attributes;
he keeps his cards in place.
But best of all, he sure knows how
to keep a poker face.

"But when it comes to serious poker,
he's far down on the scale.
Whenever he gets a real good hand,
he wags his doggoned tail!"

THE DEAD HORSE
Tony Ilardi

The ranch boss, Jim Ryan,
bought a stallion named Red.
One hell of a horse,
so the auctioneer said.

He paid a high price,
but this horse he could scoot,
and Jim knew that in time
Red would bring him some loot.

One day Jim had to leave
to buy some new stock.
He worried about Red
'cause he sure was in hock.

He put Bill in charge
while he was away.
He said, "Take care of Red, Bill,
and watch he don't stray!"

Then several days later,
when Jim he called home,
the telephone rang and
Bill answered the phone.

"Bill, how's Red a-doin'?
Are you keeping him fed?"
But Bill answered, "No!"
He said, "Red turned up dead!"

Well, Jim started cussin';
he said, "That's a hell of a way
to give me bad news
when I'm this far away!

"You should have told me
that old Red got tangled
in the barbed-wire fence
and he really got mangled!

"Then when I called back to check,
you could say, 'Boss, I won't lie.
We got the best vet
but he said Red might die!'

"When I called a third time,
you could say with a frown,
'Boss, we did what we could,
but Doc put old Red down!'

"When you got some bad news,
break it gently, Bill.
Think of folks' feelings
and you won't make 'em ill!"

Bill said, "Jim, I'm sure sorry!
I just didn't think!
A bad shock like that
could make a man drink!

"I got some more news
that you might want to know.
You'd better sit down;
this will come as a blow!

"Jim, your wife she got tangled
in that very same wire.
But we're working like hell
to try and untie her!"

Bill Jones
Lander, Wyoming

Bill wrangles dudes, writes a column for the *Wyoming State Journal*, hosts a weekly cowboy radio show, and says, "My heroes have always been cowboys. I am living a dream." He likes the independence of the ranching lifestyle, and writes his poems based on those real-life experiences. "'Little Slim' is an old story my Dad told me when I was about eight years old. A lot of my poems are classic old jokes put to verse."

LITTLE SLIM

"Late again," the third-grade teacher
Said to Little Slim.
(When anyone was late for school,
It usually was him.)

"It ain't my fault, Miss Addy,
You can blame this on my Pa.
The reason I'm three hours late?
Pa sleeps nights in the raw!"

Now Miss Addy had taught grammar school
For thirty-some-odd years.
So she asked Slim what he meant by that,
Despite her mounting fears.

Full of grin and mischief,
In the flower of his youth,
Slim and Trouble were ol' pards—
But he always told the truth.

"You see, Miss Addy, at the ranch
This here lowdown coyote
The last few nights done et six hens
And killed Ma's best milk goat.

"And last night when Pa heard a noise
Out in the chicken pen,
He grabbed his gun and said to Ma,
'That coyote's back again.'

" 'Stay back,' he yelled to all us kids,
'I wouldn't want ya hurt!'
He was naked as a jaybird—
No boots, no pants, no shirt!

"To the henhouse on all fours he crawled
Like an Injun on the snoop.
Then he stuck the double barrel
Through the window of the coop.

"As he stared into the darkness,
With coyotes on his mind,
Our ol' hound Zeke had done woke up
And come sneakin' up behind.

"Then we all looked on plumb helpless
As Pa was cold-nosed without warnin'.
Miss Addy, we been cleanin' chickens
Since three o'clock this mornin'!"

THE COOK'S REVENGE
Bill Jones

Cookin' ain't no easy job,
If anyone should ask.
And cookin' for a cowboy crew
Is a downright thankless task.

"The grub is cold," the boys will say,
Or else, "There's too much salt."
Any blame to pass around,
You can bet it's all my fault.

The eggs get broke and the biscuits burn,
The griddle won't get hot.
Try bakin' apple pie sometime
When apples you ain't got.

One day I fixed some French cuisine,
Served fancy wine and such;
The boys all held their guts and moaned
They didn't like it much.

The boss, he held his plate aloft
Like he'd fished it from a sewer.
The boys described my gourmet meal
With a word that means "manure."

They hurt my pride, them cowboys did,
I almost walked away.
But then again, revenge is sweet—
There'd be another day.

The answer finally came to me
In the middle of a drunk;
I'd make them ignorant cowboys pay—
I'd feed them boys a skunk.

So I found an old dead polecat
Layin' in the road,
Boiled him up one afternoon,
Threw in a horny toad.

I piled their tin plates high that night,
But much to my surprise
Them dad-burned heathens ate it all—
I could not believe my eyes.

I started once to tell 'em
The whole thing was a joke,
But they were belchin' so contentedly
And had rared back for a smoke.

"Cookie" they said gleefully,
"You finally learned to cook.
Can I have the recipe?
Did you get it from a book?"

Them cowboys had no idea,
And they ain't found out yet
They was feastin' on some critters
That ought not to be et.

Yep, cookin' is a real tough job;
It ain't no easy life.
And if my food you just can't eat,
Well . . . be glad I ain't your wife.

THE PRETZEL HOLD

Bill Jones

There was this well-known wrestler
Who had won Olympic gold,
And he rose to fame and fortune
With what was called the "Pretzel Hold."
He would twist his poor opponent
In a mass of arms and legs
And reduce him to a helpless mass
Of whines and moans and begs.

He soon became World Champion
(All agreed he was the best),
And his manager arranged a tour
Down through the Great Southwest,
Where this little Texas Cowboy
(Who thought that he was tough)
Said, "That Pretzel feller ain't so hot,
And I've heard about enough!
And I'll rassle that there braggart,
If he's inclined to fight,
In Houston's great big Astrodome
This comin' Friday night."

Well, they turned out by the thousands
To watch the cowboy lose.
They dressed him in some baggy drawers
And them silly-lookin' shoes.
Then the Champ turned plumb ferocious
At the first sound of the bell,
Then commenced to teach the cowboy
'Bout the "hold" conceived in hell.

He knotted up his arms and legs;
They both fell to the mat.
The fans gave a collective sigh—
That was the end of that.
But wait! Could this be happening?

Our cowboy's on his feet!
Why, he's got the Pretzel Feller pinned!
The Champ has jest been beat!

The crowd erupts in wild applause,
Whistles, shouts, and cheers!
This is the greatest upset win
In forty-seven years.
Well, things they finally settle down,
The fans they all go home,
And the cowboy and his trainer Dad
Are left there in the Dome.

"It's a miracle," the old man says,
"I can't believe you won!
But I got one naggin' question:
How did you do it, son?"
"Well, he had me in that Pretzel Hold
And I knew that things was bad—
It was the most excruciating
PAIN I ever had.

"And as we laid there in that tangle
Of arms and legs and toes,
I seen this pair of 'family jewels'
A-swingin' by my nose.
I figgered it my only chance,
I had to win the fight,
So I grabbed a double mouthful
And then took a great big bite."

"So, that's it!" the old man cries,
"I see now what you mean—
That explains the biggest victory
That I have *ever* seen!"
"One more thing," the cowboy says,
" 'Tween us and these here walls . . .
A man don't know what pain is
'Til he chomps on his own balls!"

LeRoy Jones
Mountain View, Oklahoma

Raised in a ranching/farming family, LeRoy has continued that lifestyle himself. He has participated in cowboy poetry gatherings in nine different states, and serves as an Artist in Residence with the State Arts Council of Oklahoma. Of his lifestyle he says, "Working with the land and cattle is not an easy life but is a rewarding one. I only wish the rewards were bankable at the First National."

I'M WORKING FOR THE GOVERNMENT

I'm working on the barn one day and going at a run.
The tin had started coming loose; the nails had come undone.
With weathermen predicting rain, the wind was on the rise.
I knew I had to finish up this little enterprise,

When I just caught a glimpse of something coming past the shop.
It drove right up beside the barn and skidded to a stop.
And ritzier than any rig I'd ever seen before—
This shiny new Suburban with some writing on the door.

The driver shut the engine off, and then for just a bit
He shuffled through some papers and I watched until he quit.
And climbing down from off the barn so I could meet this gent,
I saw the writing on the door said U.S. GOVERNMENT.

The driver then steps out and I can say without dispute,
He looked a little out of place there in his business suit.
His hat and tie and shiny shoes all led me to conclude
That, brother, judging by his looks, this fellow was a dude.

"I'm P. J. Finklemeyer," he said and caught me off my guard,
'Cause when I reached to shake his hand he handed me his card.
"Now Mister Jones, I'll tell you what this visit is about.
I'm working for the government. I'm here to help you out.

"You see, I've been commissioned to go out across the land
And draw upon my expertise, to lend a helping hand—
Evaluate your operation, then to plan the change
That's needed if you want to keep your home out on the range."

He said if I would spend the day and show him 'round the place
That he could give me counsel, and that great big empty space
Could soon bring forth abundantly a crop of different sort.
He'd motioned to the pasture where the grass was getting short.

The kind of help I needed didn't look to be his kind.
A plan of operation wasn't what I had in mind.
At branding time I needed help, and also making hay,
And I could use 'bout twenty hours of daylight every day.

But this young bantam rooster just kept crowing on and on
The way a rooster always does in heralding the dawn.
I couldn't turn him off it seemed, no matter how I tried.
He had the world all figured out, and he sure testified.

I said, "If you'll excuse me, maybe you have just begun.
But this here job I've started, I've just got to get it done.
Feel free to go out on your own and look till you're content,
But I can't take the time to join in your experiment."

"But surely you can spare the time to help enrich your life.
Consider all your children, and just think about your wife.
Why, you could all be better off with just my good advice.
The way you operate this place is terrible," he cries.

But when I started work again, he left me in a huff
And muttered loud enough to hear a lot of unkind stuff,
Like "dumb cowboys" and "stupid farmers," "aggies and the lot
Not recognizing genius," and some that I forgot.

I tried to put him from my mind and went about my chore
And didn't even think of him for 'bout an hour or more,
Until I heard this urgent cry come riding on the breeze.
Why, could that be a call for help? and was he saying please?

The sound was getting louder so I had myself a look.
I poked my head around the barn and laughed until I shook.
This dude was running for a tree, a bull in hot pursuit,
And super quick he climbed that tree, there in his three-
    piece suit.

And as he sat there on a limb, the bull below his feet
A-pawing and a-snorting, he just didn't look so neat.
His tie was flapping in the wind, his britches leg was ripped.
For handling bulls and climbing trees he hadn't come equipped.

As soon as he composed himself a bit I heard him say,
"Oh, Mister Jones, would you please come and drive this
    bull away?
He isn't very friendly and I fear he'll do me harm.
He doesn't seem to understand I've come to help your farm.

"I'm working for the government, I'm here to give you aid,
But now I've got myself into a pickle I'm afraid.
So would you come and help me out? This limb is getting hard."
As calmly as I could I said, "Just show the bull your card."

THE PREACHER'S HORSE

LeRoy Jones

The Preacher saw this Cowhand come a-walking up the lane—
His saddle on his shoulder and his face was marked with pain.
The Preacher said, "Just come right in and pull you up a chair
And tell me of the problem that has brought you to despair."

The Cowboy said, "My horse stepped in a hole and took a fall,
It broke his leg and so I had to shoot him. After all,
You can't just let them suffer, but it fills me with remorse
To take his life that way; but, Preacher, now I need a horse."

The Preacher said, "You're lucky, 'cause I've got just what
    you need.
I trained a horse for my own use, but I'll sell you that steed.
He's sound as any dollar, and he's up to any task,
You'll find him plenty willing, and he'll give you all you ask.

"Come out and take a look at him and see if you agree
He'll do for what you have in mind. He's good, I guarantee."
The chance to get a horse like that sure boosted his morale,
So he got up with the Preacher and went to the corral.

That Preacher knew his horses, that was very plain to see;
So they both struck a bargain for a reasonable fee.
The Preacher said, "You've bought the best and that I'll verify.
But let me tell you one more thing before you say good-bye.

"I trained that horse to use myself and taught him by the Book.
For you to use him here's the rules you mustn't overlook.
He works by voice command alone; your guard you mustn't drop,
'Cause Giddap doesn't make him go, and Whoa don't make
    him stop.

"I trained him with the words I use in sermons that I preach,
So you just need to learn these words and proper use of each.

To make him go, say 'Praise the Lord.' He'll move right out,
    and then,
Just when you want to make him stop you simply say, 'Amen.'

"With just a bit of practice you can learn that in no time.
These words will make him hit a run, or stop him on a dime."
So this Cowpuncher saddled up and then he climbed aboard,
And making this small clicking sound said, "ck, ck, Praise the Lord!"

The horse stepped out and in a canter headed down the lane.
He said, "Amen," and then the horse came to a stop again.
Why this would be more simple than he even dared to hope,
And with that knowledge, shouting "Praise the Lord," he hit a lope.

With fluid motion horse and rider seemed to be as one—
The distance simply fell away. That horse could truly run.
The Cowpoke didn't seem to know how far he'd really gone
Until amazed he saw the cleft that he had come upon.

He knew it was the river with a bluff on either side,
And knew if he went over he had taken his last ride.
"Whoa, horse!" he shouted and pulled back with all his might,
But that horse didn't break his stride or slow his headlong flight.

Now what was it the Preacher said that he would have to say
To make that horse come to a stop, now did he say to pray?
That's not quite it. Oh, now I know. "AMEN," he fairly shrieked
And brought him to a sliding stop—but he could hardly speak.

His heart was right up in his throat and pounding like a drum,
And he could barely catch his breath, the scare left him so numb.
The bluff edge there was right back underneath the horse's chin.
How lucky he remembered that he had to say "Amen."

He stood up in his stirrups there and looked down at the bluff.
There wasn't room for one more step. Man, that was close enough!
He'd almost met his maker and collected his reward.
He sunk back in the saddle as he sighed, "Oh, Praise the Lord!"

Don Kennington
Ogden, Utah

Don shoes horses, writes and recites cowboy poetry, and helps work the family ranch for a living. He has had several poems and some horseshoeing articles published in magazines and newspapers. Don says he has been cowboying as long as he can remember and enjoys the "peace and serenity that rides the trails with me."

THE GAS CAN

Bill and Sal had a little ranch, a few cows and a saddle horse.
They needed hay for the wintertime, so they raised their own,
    of course.
They bought a tractor, mower and rake, though they were old
    and worn.
Bill said that he could fix them up and put them in the barn.

He got some tools and rags and oil and an old can full of gas.
He'd wash the parts and paint 'em up, give them a little class.
He kept that can of gas around. Sal said it smelled pretty bad.
But when she asked him to dump it out, it made him a little mad.

One day when Bill was mowing hay, she took that can of gas
And poured it down the outhouse so it wouldn't kill the grass.
Now, there were spiders in the outhouse and underneath the porch,
So when Bill went to the privy, he'd light a paper torch.

He'd run that torch around the hole to scare the spiders away,
Then he'd sit down in comfort in his little hideaway.
Well that night after supper, Bill grabbed some paper and a match;
He headed on back to the outhouse and closed the indoor latch.

He dropped his pants around his feet and lit his paper wand,
And waved it at the spiders like a majorette's baton.
Now about a half a mile away the neighbors were having a fight.
Minnie said, "Sam, you drunken fool, you'll meet your doom
    all right."

He was pushing on the door while she was holding fast.
He was mumbling under his breath when they heard that
    fateful blast.
The neighbors on the other side were looking at the sky
About the time Bill lit the paper and the outhouse went bye-bye.

The first that went was the outhouse roof and then the door
    and walls;
Then the catalog from Sears Roebuck and the seat with two
    round stalls.
You know, it was the oddest thing, that seat a-floatin' around,
Like someone there with glasses on a-surveyin' the ground.

There were boards and hinges and other stuff raining all over
    the place.
It woke the chickens and scared the hogs; there was fear on
    Sally's face.
The neighbors said the fireworks were something to behold,
And the mower and the tractor got splattered up with mold.

People said it sounded like a Chinese holiday,
But the stuff that fell from out the sky ruined all the hay.
When they found the catalog, lying open at the bathroom page,
It said that indoor toilets are now the going rage.

Well, Sam ain't touched a drop of booze since that explosive night
When Ol' Bill blew the outhouse up an' made his solo flight.
And Bill, he's doing better now, his eyebrows are growing back.
He still sits on a cushion though—goose feathers in a gunnysack.

The neighbors rebuilt the outhouse, and Sal, she's moved back home.
Sam and Minnie seem happy now that he leaves the booze alone.
When I think back to that night and mull it over in my mind,
It's hard to get the picture straight—get the sequence to unwind.

Bill must have been up there somewhere, tho' I can't say for sure.
The flash of gas and the dark of night made visibility poor.
Something else was different, too—the thing that caught my eye,
That's the only time I ever saw two moons in the same night sky.

Phil Kennington
Sandy, Utah

Phil shoes horses for a living and works on the family cattle ranch on the Wyoming-Idaho border. He has coauthored three books, and has a poem published monthly in *Horse Sense*. Of his lifestyle he says, "The fun of rodeo life, the freedom of range life, and the fundamentals of ranch life seem to hold a fascination of basic simplicity where one controls his/her own destiny."

THE COWBOY AND THE SEAGULL

Now the judge he wuzn't happy
    When they brought the cowboy in.
The charge wuz "Seagull Poachin'."
    It wuz time for discipline.

It wuz time to teach that feller
    That we all should coexist,
Or else seagulls might end up
    On the endangered species list.

And so the judge demanded
    Jake explain the reason why
The environment got trampled
    And that seagull had to die.

Jake said, "I's lost out on the prairie,
    Sees this bird up in a tree.
I hadn't et fer days.
    It wuz either him er me."

The old judge felt compassion.
    The cowboy seemed sincere.
Said he'd join the "Save A Seagull Club"
    And be a volunteer.

And so the judge dismissed the case.
    To pursue it seemed a waste.
And then he said, "Jake, by the way,
    Just how does seagull taste?"

Jake answered, "Oh, it's similar
    To any other fowl.
It's a little like bald eagle,
    But it's more like spotted owl."

ROCKET
Phil Kennington

Ole Rocket had distemper,
He was sick and wet with sweat.
He gave a groan, I grabbed the phone
But couldn't reach the vet.

The vet had left this great big pill
The last time he was out.
Said it was sure to heal and cure,
'Twas strong with lots of clout.

Ole Rocket got cantankerous
And he wouldn't take the pill.
The stubborn steed, I could see we'd need
To go against his will.

I cuts three feet of garden hose
To thread down Rocket's throat.
He took the hose when we twitched his nose
But it sorta got his goat.

I popped that big pill in my mouth
To blow it thru the hose.
That horse will get that big pill yet
With one of my big blows.

I took a big breath in
'Til I thought my lungs would burst,
But the horse had skill, I took the pill
'Cuz Rocket, he blowed first.

THE LOST COW
Phil Kennington

Now Jed had lost his hearing
    And he'd also lost his cow,
And he'd hunted hill and hollow,
    But he'd lost her trail somehow.

So Jed, he asked the preacher
    To recruit some help at church.
The preacher said he'd ask for men
    To help him with his search.

So Sunday from the pulpit
    Came the call for volunteers.
Jed told 'em that his cow was black
    With white around both ears.

Said, "Ya could spot her easy
    'Cause both her horns turned up.
She'll answer when she hears her name—
    She's called ole 'Buttercup'."

Then Jed described her, horn to tail,
    His picture left no doubt,
And they organized a big cow hunt
    To start when church was out.

The preacher had one more concern
    Before his Sunday text,
And he checked his church agenda
    To determine what was next.

He announced a brand new member,
    Widder Jones was asked to stand.
Then the congregation offered
    Widder Jones a welcome hand.

And several stood to testify
    They'd heard that Widder Jones
Could sing a fine soprano,
    That she even played the bones.

Some claimed they'd heard she even preached,
    That she was full of fire,
And with open arms they welcomed
    Widder Jones into the choir.

Now Jed, he thought that they wuz
    Still a-talkin' 'bout his cow,
And he remembered some things
    He'd forgotten up 'til now.

And so he stood again,
    And everybody held their breath,
And Lula Hawkins claims what happened
    Next was worse than death.

Jed said, "She ain't much fer purty,
    She won't make no record books—
With boney hips and fat thick lips,
    She's older than she looks.

"Her favorite food is watercress,
    She'll slobber when she eats,
'Cause her teeth are chopped and broken,
    And she's got more fat than meat."

He said, "She's frothy at the mouth,
    And her breath gets pretty bad,
And she's noisy when she's drinkin',
    And she bellers when she's mad."

Now the church was deathly quiet,
    Not ONE amen could be heard,
And everyone was hopin'
    Jed had spoke the final word . . .

The deacon whispered in Jed's ear
    When the congregation froze.
For all it solved he might as well
    Have whispered in his nose.

Well, Jed appeared to understand;
    He turned and faced the crowd.
And since he couldn't hear himself
    His voice came harsh and loud:

"She likes to run in sagebrush
    And when she's wet she's smelly.
Her left ear's split and she's lost one teat,
    And the hair's rubbed off her belly."

A Cowboy Goes to Town
Phil Kennington

For sixty years I'd been content.
    I'd never been to town.
Just ridin' horses, herdin' cows—
    I'd really settled down.

But when we got the oil well,
    The family said that I should spy
The sights of Houston town
    Just once before I die.

I reared back like a balky horse
    'Cause I had always heard
That city folks ain't friendly much,
    And I b'lieved every word.

But now I know that just ain't so;
    I flat out disagrees.
I got more friends in Houston now
    Than a cow dog has got fleas.

With steer horns mounted on the hood
    Of a brand new Cadillac,
I'm makin' tracks to Houston town
    And I ain't lookin' back.

No shiftin' gears like the old John Deers,
    I let out a groan.
I like to got a whiplash
    When it shifted on its own.

A buzzard had his head down where
    He'd found some fresh roadkill.
He's goin' to Houston with me now
    Spread-eagle on the grill.

We hit the city limits.
    The road sign said, "One Way."
One way's all I planned on goin',
    So I figures I'm O.K.

And that's when I first noticed
    Them folks' hospitality.
They'd wave when I come t'wards 'em,
    And even call to me.

They'd wave both arms and holler
    And I'd yell, "Howdy" back
While flyin' down that one-way street
    In my brand new Cadillac.

They liked my steer horns best of all.
    They'd yell, "Watch out, cowboy."
I'm wavin' back to all my friends
    And they shake their fists with joy.

The Sheriff roars up on my left.
    We're drivin' parallel.
And then he waves me over 'cuz
    He wants to chat a spell.

He said, "You goin' to a fire
    In that hopped-up Cadillac?"
I said, "The fire must be over,
    Everybody's comin' back."

He got plumb enthusiastic,
    And he's showin' me his gun.
He's jumpin' and a-shoutin'.
    He wuz havin' lots of fun.

He showed me all his flashin' lights.
    I said, "They DO look good."
And I showed him my steer horns
    I had mounted on my hood.

He stared in utter silence,
    And he wuz real impressed.
I said, "Your Christmas lights ARE purty,
    But I likes my steer horns best."

Then he got the Christmas Spirit
    When he heard me mention it,
And he gave me one free ticket
    So that I could come and visit

The Judge's Court in Houston
    Before the twenty-third.
And I thanked him for the honor
    'Cause he got me registered.

The folks in Houston think I'm great.
    Our friendship's just begun.
They honk and point one finger
    'Cause they think I'm number ONE!

THE SKUNK AND THE COWBOYS
Phil Kennington

At the gatherin' in St. Anthony,
    A place my heart belongs,
They're spinnin' ropes and tellin' jokes
    And singin' cowboy songs.

Oh, there was lots of poetry,
    Both humorous and sad.
But this year's theme was different,
    Variation was the fad.

They even had a contest goin'
    At the city square.
A skunk-corralled tent
    And skunk scent filled the air.

The contest rules were simple 'cuz
    A hundred dollars went
To the man who stayed the longest
    With the skunk inside the tent.

When we sees that easy money there,
    We slaps our knees with glee.
Then me and Bob and Charley,
    We paid our entry fee.

Charley goes in first and
    Twenty seconds goes by fast.
But when I hears him coughin',
    Then I knows that he won't last.

He wuz wheezin' and a-gaspin'.
    We could hear him cuss and swear.
Then both tent flaps flew open wide
    And Charley dove for air.

He hit the ground a-rollin',
    Ya could see him agonize.
There wuz tears as big as biscuits
    Runnin' down from both his eyes.

Well, I'm up next, I figures
    That it can't be bad as death.
I grit my teeth and shut my eyes
    And try to hold my breath.

I can hear the judge a-countin'
    As he gets to twenty-five.
And I'm gettin' weak and dizzy but
    At least I'm still alive.

Then I staggers t'wards the tent flaps.
    This is more than I can bear.
I might just die a loser,
    But I gotta have some air.

I sucks air in for all I'm worth.
    I wheeze and cough and spit,
Then dives out like an arrow
    Just beyond where Charley lit.

We shoulda knowed Bob had the edge.
    He held an ace or two;
Didn't have a wife or mother
    To tell him what to do.

He wuz sorta used to odors—
    Not the kind from hollyhocks,
But them ya find when ya ain't changed
    Yer underwear and sox.

He weren't opposed to changin' clothes,
    Although it made him stout.
But puttin' 'em on and takin' 'em off
    He claims just wears 'em out.

Oh, sometimes Bob bathed in the spring—
    He figured that would do.
But the last time he bathed in spring
    Was the spring of sixty-two.

And so when Bob went in the tent
    To try and win the prize,
And beat out me and Charley
    It was really no surprise.

When the seconds ticked by quietly
    The tent was calm and still,
And it looks like me and Charley'd
    Lost that hundred-dollar bill.

Then both tent flaps flew open wide,
    And now things really stunk.
And holdin' his nose with both paws
    Comes that wheezin', gaggin' skunk!

COWBOY GRANOLA
Phil Kennington

I'm a-startin' this poem just the other day.
　　My wife's in the kitchen when I hears her say,
"I've been a-readin' your notes and, lucky for you,
　　I've discovered an error or two."

Well, the only error that I'd ever known
　　Was them like Geronimo shot from his bow.
But my wife, she's from Boston, so I thought it best
　　To give her a listen since I'm from the West.

The schools in the city are better, I hear.
　　They learn you to talk proper and write so it's clear.
Said she'd edit my poem if I agreed
　　To read it back to her—so I proceed.

"Cowboy Granola, copyright April 1994.

" 'Twas up in a line shack, the first fall of snow—
　　A couple of mice hadn't no place to go."
"Now hold it right there, cowboy," she cried.
　　"That's a double negative." I swell with pride.

I said, "I'm glad that ya like it. I figured ya would.
　　But I had no idea you'd like it that good."
Her mouth is wide open. I thought she might yawn.
　　Her stare seemed impressive and so I read on.

"On the shelf in the line shack was dried beans and rice,
　　And it was discovered by that pair of mice.
So when eatin' granola, 'might think on it twice.
　　It was co-invented by cowboys and mice.

"On the shelf in the line shack, the mice did their share,
   'Cause they contributed more than just hair."
My wife yells, "That's gross!" I know *gross* means *a lot.*
   I said, "Thank you kindly, that is a good spot.

"Especially what's happenin' up there on the shelf.
   I was sorta favorin' that part myself."
She says I wouldn't know the difference between
   A past participle and her sewing machine.

But I know participles. I've studied their ways.
   Even shot one back when I was huntin' for strays.
She said, "An encyclopedia is what you need.
   And the sooner the better." But I disagreed.

Don't need no cyclopedia and I told her so.
   My pickup will get me where I wanna go.
She says to me, "Cowboy, you don't even know
   That most cowboy lingo's from Old Mexico.

"There's mesa, remuda, and tapadero;
   Latigo, pinto, and sombrero;
Chaparo, vaquero, and hot jumpin' beans.
   You don't even know what the word 'Spanish' means."

I let her know I'm plenty smart about treats.
   Said, "Spanish is that stuff that old Popeye eats."
She says, "I speak Spanish and English, too.
   So I am bilingual." I says, "Bully for you!

"If you're a bilingualist that suits me fine.
   You go to your church and I'll go to mine."

SHOTGUN CHAPS
Phil Kennington

We was headin' toward the home ranch,
    Gatherin' cattle every day.
They seemed to know there'd soon be snow
    And they'd be needin' hay.

The boss's oldest daughter, Sue,
    Was often on my mind.
But if I'd known what lay ahead,
    I'd left sweet Sue behind.

That episode plumb wrecked my life.
    'Twas one of nature's traps.
It was the first and only time
    That I wore shotgun chaps.

I'd been a-wearin' bat wings;
    They buckled in the back.
Two snaps around each leg
    And it was time to make yer track.

But them shotgun chaps was different.
    Ya put 'em on like pants.
Ya buckled 'em up in front,
    And ya could do it in a trance.

We was up long 'afore daybreak,
    Still too dark to see a cow.
I'd forgot about them shotgun chaps—
    Won't need 'em anyhow.

I slid into my Levi's; 'least I THOUGHT
    That's what they wuz.
Then I saddled up ole Joe
    Just like I always does.

Well, the saddle felt a little cold.
    I shoulda noticed then.
The contact took my breath away;
    Raised up then down again.

The saddle seemed some warmer now,
    And I was sittin' low.
My attention on the cattle
    Tryin' to get 'em up to go.

Well, we got the herd together,
    We'd be eatin' on the trail;
And the boss's wife and daughters
    Would be bringin' out the mail.

The stars seemed to be winkin'
    At each other in the sky.
The moon was sorta smilin'
    And I was wonderin' why.

I could hear the old chuck wagon
    A-bringin' up the drag,
And beyond, some female voices,
    And the whinny of a nag.

'Twas about my turn for breakfast.
    I'd ride in and grab some chuck,
Arrivin' with them women folks—
    Now how 'bout that for luck.

It was almost daylight now,
    And I put the spurs to Joe.
As I charged up to them womenfolk
    I yelled, "GERONIMO!"

The womenfolk, they all screamed, too.
    I thought I'd made a hit
'Til I looked where they wuz lookin',
    And my heart and liver quit.

Well, my romance with Sue was through.
    Guess I came on a bit too fast.
Just stick to cows and horses now.
    Glad that's all in the past.

Well, I left the territory
    Headin' southbound on old Joe.
I can't forget the way we met.
    I'd like to missed that show.

I'd like to ride up north again.
    Someday I may, perhaps;
But if I do I'm tellin' you.
    I'm wearin' bat-wing chaps.

C. Duane Kerr
Tremonton, Utah

Duane grew up on a family farm in Tremonton and eventually practiced medicine and surgery in that town for twenty-five years. He says he didn't really like poetry until he heard cowboy poetry. Now he's written over fifty works of cowboy poetry, published two books, and given over 150 performances. "The Cowboy Goes to College" was his first poem.

THE COWBOY GOES TO COLLEGE

This cowboy got a letter from his girlfriend back in town;
Said she was goin' away to college, gonna earn a cap and gown.
He heard from her 'most every week—least for a week or two;
Then there was a long dry spell, and he wondered what to do.

Then shortly after Christmas he heard from her agin;
Said she felt she had to write to him to tell him she'd been pinned.
Then weeks went by without a word; concern began to hatch.
Why should she quit writing just 'cause she lost a rasslin' match?

He thought it funny anyway, she'd take a rasslin' class.
She'd always seemed so feminine, such a dainty lass.
Then he had a bright idea, inspired by love, no doubt:
He'd take a college course himself, at the same time check her out.

They said he'd have to register, which he was glad to do.
He had a papered quarter horse; now he'd be papered, too.
So he mailed in his pedigree to the college on the hill;
Said his lineage was uncertain, but his folks were married still.

"Send a transcript of your credits," was the next thing that
      they asked.
But he didn't need no credit; he always paid in cash.
They asked about a scholarship; he said, "Thank you," in a note.
He planned to take his pickup; didn't think he'd need a boat.

They mailed him a catalog and a thick class schedule, too.
He studied them for hours and hours to see what he should do.
He had to search to find a class that seemed to fit his goal.
Then he found a class called "Fencing" and decided to enroll.

And then there was another class, might help him in the fall,
And so he signed the dotted line for "University Chorale."
Now he'd built a lot of fences and corrals he'd worked on, too;
But what the heck, he might as well get an up-to-date review

Of the latest information
On his favorite vocation.
So with brave anticipation,
He went to get an education.

So the cowboy left for college; in his pickup truck he went.
Figured since they had a campus there'd be room to pitch a tent.
But they put him in a building that they called a dormitory,
With a bunch of guys of every size and every category.

He saw this row of houses with a brand on every door,
But they was all strange letters that he'd never seen before.
No Lazy K, no Rockin' J, no Quarter Circle C.
Said he, "I've never seen them brands; they all look Greek to me."

When he signed up for this fencin' class, they said he'd need a foil,
So he brought a roll of Reynolds Wrap, and his fencin' tool, all oiled.
Them fencers were queer-lookin'; their pants all seemed too tight.
Instead of buildin' fences, they all brought swords to fight.

The class called "University Chorale" still offered upward movement
For a ranch hand from the mountains set on vocational
    improvement.
So to the Fine Arts Building all his buildin' tools he brings,
To a classroom full of college kids who just stand around and sing.

He sat through his first lecture, but before the hour was spent,
He knew without a question what the letters "B.S." meant.
All of them professors had degrees behind their names,
And he very soon concluded "M.S." meant "more of the same."
It didn't take much longer 'til it was plain to see
That "piled up higher and deeper" was what was meant by "Ph.D."

At last his first day ended; he was really feelin' blue.
He felt like he'd been stomped on; needed something fun to do.
His roommates learned he'd played some poker; asked him to
    teach them, too.
He figured now he knew enough to teach a thing or two.

So they started playin' poker; he was still a-feelin' sore.
But as the game progressed he reckoned he could even up
    the score.
Before the sun come up next morning, he had taught them
    how to play,
And all his roommates were flat broke and started gripin'
    in dismay.
"You said you'd teach us poker—all the rules and how to play.
You didn't say before the game how much we'd have to pay."

"Whoa now, just a minute," said the cowboy from the sticks.
"It wasn't like a swindler tried to scam a bunch of hicks.
You college boys, you must have known, before your shirts you lost,
Any education that you get is darn sure goin' to cost."

E. J. Kirchoff
Coos Bay, Oregon

With his own outfit on the Oregon coast for fifty-five years, E.J. grew up in the days of bunkhouse poets and storytellers and "can't remember anything beyond horses." He's had several poems published in magazines and newspapers, and has also written and illustrated eleven books of poetry.

LOST HORSE

We're there in Wilbur's stable
Passin' of the time away.
Old Smokey Jones says, "I been
Huntin' horses gone astray.

"I done a lot a ridin'
'Fore I got 'em back agin.
But still had one horse missin'
When I got 'em in the pen.

"I saddled up next mornin'
And went out to hunt some more.
I run across Big Chief. He said,
'Man, what ya lookin' for?'

"I said, 'I'm lookin' for a horse
I'm wantin' now to use.
He is a dandy cuttin' horse.
Ain't one I want to lose.'

"Big Chief said, 'Maybe him I see.
Dat horse, am him a black?
Short tail? And do him have two
Saddle marks upon him back?

"'A piebald with a lotta white
A-showin' 'round him eye?
Do him have two front stockin's
Dat both reach up pretty high?

"'And do him have a short white sock
On each foot dere behind?
How much you gonna pay me
If dat horse me go and find?'

"I said, 'I ain't about to buy
A horse belongs to me.'
Chief said, 'Too bad you lose dat horse.
Dat horse me sure no see.'"

SMART DOGS
E. J. Kirchoff

The talk in Wilbur's stable
Was of dogs that fellers had.
Was some sure dandy good ones
And some others that were bad.

Old Smokey Jones said, "Whippersnapper
Is the best old dog
I've ever had for herdin' cows
Or movin' of a hog."

Old Deacon said, "That Komadore
I got for guardin' sheep
Sure keeps away the kiotes,
And I don't lose any sleep."

Another feller had a dog
Was good for huntin' bear.
Another had a dandy
Puttin' pheasants in the air.

Old Bill said, "Reckon Shaggerboy
Is smart as any are.
He always likes to bark when
Someone drives up in a car.

"And in the house he likes to park
Right in my easy chair.
I'd just go to the window
When I'd want him outa there

"And say, 'A car's a-comin'.
Wonder what they're comin' for.'
And he'd jump down off my chair
And go a-barkin' for the door.

"Then I would take my easy chair
And ketch up on the news—
A-readin' of the paper,
Or perhaps I'd take a snooze.

"The other day I'm restin',
Relaxed in my easy chair.
That dog runs to the window
And he goes to barkin' there.

"Well, I got up to look.
Wasn't no one comin' there.
I turned around, and that dang dog
Was in my easy chair."

John "Jay" Kulm
Chinook, Washington

John used to produce hay and grain for feedlots and dairies, and now makes his living performing cowboy poetry. He says some of his best poetry hits him while he's driving a tractor. He also gets his inspiration from watching the stars at night and "talking things out. They're good listeners."

A GIANT FOUR-POINT BUCK

In a meadow next to a graveled road on game department land,
There stood a giant four-point buck right in the palm of my hand.

I had my rifle loaded and the animal in my sights,
When a station wagon drove up to me—a man, his kids, and wife.

This family started pointing and taking pictures, too,
I put the rifle in my truck, what else was I to do?

The man said to me, "What you've just done was a kind and
    gentle act,"
I said, "My house is down the road, I guess I'll just go back."

That station wagon drove by my place that afternoon at three,
I smiled and waved at the family, they smiled and waved at me.

But I'm not too proud of how I cussed in the front yard where
    I stood,
When I saw my giant four-point buck tied down to the
    auto's hood.

Mike Logan
Helena, Montana

Fifteen years of photographing the beautiful rhythms of ranch life led Mike to try and capture its natural meter and rhyme in words as well as on film. A host and featured poet in Elko, he has recited his poetry all over the western United States and Canada. Mike is the author and photographer of three books of photography and verse and three books and tapes of cowboy poetry.

COWBOY CRUISE CONTROL

These boys, they ain't plumb housebroke yet,
Ain't used t' modern ways.
They've read about them rodeos,
The money that they pays.

Them stories in the *Horseman*
Has hooked 'em right enough.
The champ, he's just a little squirt.
It cain't be all that tough.

So ridin' off the rimrocks,
They thinks they'll do 'er right.
They'll get a brand new travel van
An' save on airplane flight.

They stops at this here RV place
An' sees this fancy van.
In less time than a doggin' run,
Up pops this new car man.

This feller, he's plumb friendly;
He's grinnin' like a whelp.
He howdies 'em like long-lost pards—
Cain't hardly wait t' help.

That van, it's got them captain's seats,
A well-stocked little bar
An' lots of shiny doodads.
They ain't plumb shore what are.

There's two TVs, a VCR,
An' skylights overhead,
A stereo and tape deck;
It's even got a bed.

There's automatic windows;
No need to turn no crank.
An' with that car thief warnin',
It's safe as any bank.

There's readin' lights an' cruise control
An' window seats galore.
The air conditioner keeps it cool;
There's carpets on the floor.

The salesman takes 'em for a ride
Out on the interstate.
Its lanes is straight as new-built fence;
Our heroes think it's great.

He slips 'er into cruise control
An' shows 'em how to do it.
Then sits there talkin', plumb relaxed.
It's plain, ain't nothin' to it.

He shows 'em 'bout the stereo
An' that new VCR.
Claims they can see their rides played back
Just like some movie star.

So, now, they'll share the travel costs,
Hit ever' show they can.
They spend their whole life's savin's
On this chromed-up travel van.

That car man, he good-byes 'em
With handshakes all around.
An' now our future cowboy stars
Is headed out of town.

They'll hit the show in Wolf Point,
The old Wild Horse Stampede.
That new van's gassed and rarin'.
They'll try 'er out for speed.

They're headed out on Highway 3,
A road they always traveled.
But on the bend just north of town,
Things starts to come unraveled.

The boy that's drivin', he gets up
An' heads back t' the bar.
T' build hisself a whisky ditch
But he don't get that far.

'Cause when he sets that cruise control
They run right off the bend.
Before they're out of town good,
Their plans is at a end.

He never got t'build no drink.
The van's a awful wreck.
Looks like some big ol' beetle
That crashed and broke his neck.

You know that number—nine one one?
Run over quick and dial it.
Turns out that boy thought cruise control
Was automatic pilot.

B. Lynne McCarthy

Terry, Montana

Lynne and her husband, Sean, are third-generation ranchers on the place grandad settled in 1902. They raise cattle and horses, and love every minute of it, except digging postholes. She feels that by living and working a ranch you truly get to experience life, and says, "Where else can you get bucked off, kicked, and then run over by the very critter you were trying to rope?!"

WHEN COWBOYS WATER-SKI

Some friends of ours have got a boat,
One with lots of speed.
Naturally they asked us if
We'd ever water-skiied.

We met up at the lake next day
Geared up in swimming clothes,
Revealing cowboys' hide stays hid,
Just hands and face exposed.

For bare bowlegs that sprout from shorts
Shining lily white,
Somehow seem next to obscene
In afternoon sunlight.

But with whoops of, "Ride 'em, cowboy!"
And wide-brimmed hats pulled down,
One by one we took our turn,
Our friends towed us around.

That is, all but Slim, who could
Not seem to master it.
Each start his skis flew everyway
And then they'd always split.

Do or die, in puncher style,
He gripped the rope and hollered,
"Give 'er all she's got this time!
I'll just up and foller!"

That outboard roared and water flew,
Out burst our buddy, Slim;
Though he was on his skis, a new
Problem troubled him.

He'd split the waves with such a force
It waterlogged his shorts,
And put the cowboy on display
A-cussin' water sports.

It helped him ski to have his ankles
Hobbled, bound in place
By those baggy swimming trunks
That left him in disgrace.

But top hands never let a rope loose,
Not even up on skis,
So Slim just drug along behind;
He couldn't turn it free.

The boat swung past the sandy beach
Crowded with weekenders,
Which sure set ol' Slim to wishing
That he'd worn suspenders!

His bare rump flashing in the wake
Was causing quite the rush.
He looked much like an antelope
Bounding through the brush!

Now we're back at work, except for Slim,
So sunburned he can't ride.
When cowboys water-ski, they need
To cover tender hide.

Larry McWhorter
Weatherford, Texas

L
arry currently makes his living as a writer and a dayworker on local ranches. He's been published in magazines and anthologies, and has taken part in cowboy poetry gatherings all over the country. He says his work lets him enjoy the "comradery of the men who have chosen to be part of a lifestyle few will ever know or understand."

THE EXPERT

'Twas seventy-six, I think was the year
On that fateful day in the spring.
Jack Moreman took us, the pride of the school,
To see if we'd learned anything.

The Rafter O was the sight of the test.
Jay Taylor had loaned us a wad
Of three hundred heifers, all black as sin,
And each was a pea in a pod.

The course we were taking had us prepared
For the task before us that day.
Our A.I. schoolin' had give us a "feel"
For a cow in the family way.

The day was real hot, we sweated a lot
And soon reeked of something feral.
I'd spent all day long just loading the chute,
Then came my turn in the barrel.

My long glove I donned and lubed 'er up good,
The arduous task thus began.
I lifted her tail, spelunked my way in
While thinking, "This day you're a man."

The first few head I was clumsy at best
But soon I warmed up to the chore.
I'd state my findings and Jack would concur.
This lesson "I" needed no more.

Heck, this was a snap but I'm quite the chap.
Ol' Jack is real proud I believe.
I dreamed of praise and report cards with A's,
But fate had a trick up her sleeve.

After I'd tested about thirty head,
The routine had gotten so bland
That I never checked to see where I stuck
My aching, but still well-oiled, hand.

I was thinking of beer in frosty mugs,
For Sid Blues' dim lights I did long,
When I heard a cough, nay, 'twas a snicker.
I then noticed something was wrong.

This heifer was really fightin' me bad.
Though I tried with all of my might,
I couldn't get in, so I looked at Jack
And said, "Dang, but this girl is tight."

The world exploded right there in my face.
I wondered, "Now what did I do?"
Ovinely, I peeked. There was but one hole
Where I knew there should have been two.

The bomb had been dropped, I knew I'd been had,
The proverbial dunk had been slammed.
I stood there amid the laughter and jeers
But could only say, "I'll be damned."

The ride back to school was a long one, friends.
A debate I was forced to hear.
They couldn't decide who looked more surprised,
Me or that poor ol' black steer.

DRIP COFFEE
Larry McWhorter

On the day that I was married,
A present I was given
That was supposed to modernize
My archaic way of livin'.

Now don't think me ungrateful
'Cause I'll tell you that I'm not,
But I've always been suspicious
Of the slow-drip coffeepot.

For, you see, I've never trusted
Cuisine cooked by Franklin's find.
My wife said that was silly,
It was all just in my mind.

Yet one thing has always bugged me
And has caused my mind to doubt:
A feller could just starve to death
If a power pole goes out.

But it never has been said of me
I've treated things unfair,
And so one day it got its chance—
My new coffee-makin' ware.

So I filled its little basket
And poured in the water too,
Then set back and awaited
This Buck Rogers style of brew.

The aroma it emitted
Was a pleasant one, I found.
I caught myself relaxing
To its steady dripping sound.

But something here just wasn't right.
The familiar sounds I missed—
The way it boiled o'er the spout,
The friendly way it hissed.

Then suddenly it hit me!
I jumped and turned it off.
I know it's all just in my mind,
But hear me 'fore you scoff.

As I listened to its drippin',
I changed my mind 'bout switchin',
'Cause its sound was of the bathroom
And not that of the kitchen.

Scott Minor
Las Cruces, Mew Mexico

Currently attending New Mexico State University to get a degree in physical education, Scott shoes horses for a living. Like many poets, his inspiration for his poetry comes from the things he has experienced, and he tries to relate them in a way that someone who is not a cowboy can understand. An artist as well as a poet, Scott hopes to illustrate and publish his own book next year.

EASY TO FIND

Now, I've got a buddy,
he lives quite a ways from town.
I told him I was coming through;
he said be sure and come around.
"How do I get there;
will finding your place be hard?"
"Oh, no," he replied.
"It's a big brick house with a windmill in the yard."
"Not what does it look like?
I need directions," I said.
"Oh, sorry," he replied.
"Must've lost my head.
Well, first off, get on the interstate—
the one headed west—
or is it the frontage road?
No, the interstate would be best.
Go 'til you hit the exit,
the one by the river.
Get off there and turn right
or left, jeez, I can't remember.
No wait, the next exit's the one you want.

Get off there and turn right;
go 'til you hit mile marker twelve.
Turn at the cattle guard; it's big, yellow and bright.
Follow the road 'til it forks,
about eight miles south;
there's a burnt-out ranch house,
people left 'cause of some kind of drought.
Like I said, the house is burnt out,
chimney's all that's left standin';
place is pretty run down—
sure needs a lot of mendin'.
Was probably a pretty nice place once,
folks likely had a bunch of cows,
but don't go there, that's the wrong way.
Like I said, you don't want to go south.
You need to go back to the north.
I forget the number of the highway,
Fifty-five or Sixty; wish I could remember,
but I can't rightly say.
Anyway, follow it for, oh, thirty miles or so;
there'll be a billboard on your left,
something about a eatin' house
and how their food's the best.
There's a cattle guard across from it.
Cross it and go about ten miles, I guess;
you'll come to a little country store.
It's a nice place to stop and rest.
Like I said, it's a good place to coffee up
and use the bathroom if you need to,
'cause you've still got quite a ways to go
but it's a pretty scenic route.
Well, after you're relieved and coffeed back up,
go straight like you were before,
meaning the same direction you was going
when you got to that little store.

The road goes for about eighty miles
    just as straight as a string,
      but don't go too fast; there's cows on the road
      along with deer, antelope and other gamey things.
You don't want to hit one,
    could really tear up your car,
    then you'd be afoot
    and to my house it's still pretty far.
But after eighty miles or so
    you'll come to Highway Seventy.
    I know that for a fact—
    it's firmly etched in my memory.
Turn there and you'll start through the foothills;
    go about twenty miles or so,
    then go over the mountain,
    but be careful, there might still be snow.
Well, it's all downhill from there.
    The road does a switchback or two.
    I don't think there's been any rock slides lately.
    I'd sure tell you if I knew.
Once you get to the bottom,
    the ranch sits off to the right.
    Turn and go through the gate,
    the big one there made out of pipe.
It's a dirt road from there on;
    it might be a little rough.
    The county ain't real good about bladin' it.
    They make it out here about every three months.
Keep bearin' to the left
    'cause the road forks two or three times,
    but stay on the main road
    and you'll be fine.
Like I said,
    find'n this place won't be hard;
    it's a big brick house
    with a windmill in the yard.

Wayne Nelson
American Falls, Idaho

Wayne grew up on a ranch and is now a mechanic in Pocatello, Idaho. He's a member of the Cowboy Poets of Idaho and his poems have been published in magazines and anthologies. He says he's out to change the "stereotypical image of the uneducated, unworldly, hardheaded, bigoted cowboy."

SNOWVILLE

Snowville was an albino bull, a legend in his time,
His pink eyes glowed like cinders, and his horns spread sharp
    and wide,
Had hide of pure white satin that shined like Texas hail,
Except for the brand on his left hip and a green patch under the tail.

Snowville made his livin' on the circuit rodeo;
Sent them riders flyin' and the clowns runnin' to and fro.
If a rider drew old Snowville, you could bet your wrangler shirt,
You either got a high-point ride or a face full o' blood 'n' dirt.

Now Rufus'd rode his share o' bulls 'fore he became a clown,
And underneath all that makeup, that cowboy's face was brown.
The riders paid him tribute; they never put him down.
They knew their lives was in his hands once they hit the ground.

Now Rufus and ol' Snowville had done many a rodeo,
The crowds watched Snowville send that clown on many a barrel roll.
They respected one another—it was more like play than fight—
And Snowville got some extra grain behind the chutes at night.

It was in a place down south of here when Rufus was all alone,
His mouth got dry as cotton one hot old afternoon.
He walked into the nearest bar, all he wanted was a beer,
But the bouncer looks him up and down, says: "Y'ALL CAIN'T
    DRINK IN HERE!"

Now Rufus got steamed up all right; he thought he'd paid his dues.
He left that place rememberin' why his people sang the blues.
Bein' just a tad outnumbered, he left without a fight,
Headed back to the rodeo grounds and borrowed a truck that night.

Well, that honky-tonk was jumpin', with that hoorah,
    hee-haw sound,
The band was on its second break, sluggin' that bourbon down.
There was cards and dice and dancin', Wild Turkey, beer, and gin,
When the back door busted open, AND SNOWVILLE
    WANDERED IN!

History got made that night as Snowville changed the rules—
Sent the bouncer to the ladies' room, and the barmaid wet her stool;
Sent the pool table flyin', wedged up against the door,
Then knocked the lights out with his horns when he jumped
    behind the bar.

Snowville stomped and snorted, rakin' bottles off the shelves;
With his foot stuck in a spittoon, he kept time with his brass bell.
With the barkeep's apron draped across the horns above his eyes,
He spun and chased a pool shark halfway across that dive.

The barroom floor was inches deep in beer and whiskey foam,
When Snowville stopped just long enough to add a little of
    his own—
Pabst Blue Ribbon mixed with Coors, vodka mixed with draft;
He was headed for the bandstand, through it all he bucked
    and splashed.

The bass player tried to reach the door but dodged behind an amp,
As Snowville hooked the pedal steel and wore it for a hat.
The piano made a mournful honk as his tail struck a chord,
He whirled and charged that baby grand and turned it into boards.

Then Snowville stopped abruptly and made to paw the ground;
He squared off with the jukebox—it was Ernest Tubb's
    turn now—
And the colored lights exploded as him and Nashville did collide
And filled the air like fallin' rain with Top Forty forty-fives.

Well, the bouncer, he was prayin' in the second toilet stall,
As Snowville charged the mirror outside, and his head broke
    through the wall,
And the last thing he remembered (what he told the boys
    in blue)
Was this black man's face askin' him: "IS HE WHITE ENOUGH
    FOR YOU?"

Chip O'Brien
Vacaville, California

C hip has published three books of poetry and is currently working on his fourth, in addition to a collection of short stories. He's been around cowboys, ranches, and livestock (not sheep) all his life and says his ideas come from those life experiences. Chip tends to avoid crowds, but enjoys "watchin' people and writin' about the silly things they do."

SKINNY EVANS

Now, Skinny Evans, he loved rodeo;
Had a hard time to find an event.
Elbows an' knees
Was all ya could sees
Wherever that tall galoot went.

First tried his hand at bareback,
Strapped on an' they pulled the chute.
His head'd bump
On the horse's rump,
His feet dragged, an' off come his boots.

Then thought he'd try at bulldoggin',
He bailed off an' latched onto horn.
Bein' too thin
His muscles gave in;
He got folded an' spindled an' torn.

In desperation, he tried bullfightin'
An' found an event he loved dear.
When the bull tried,
He'd turn to his side,
An' ol' Skinny would plumb disappear.

FOUR PREACHERS CONFESSIN'
for Pat Ortiz
Chip O'Brien

The first one said there burned in his head
    A sinful an' hellish desire;
He wanted to dally with a woman named Sally,
    Who sang in his church's choir.

The second confessed an' he did attest
    To drinkin' more than a lot.
The whiskey an' gin was his worldly sin,
    An' that he was a drunken sot.

The third did admit when prodded a bit
    To takin' what didn't belong;
Childhood obsessions with other's possessions,
    Tho' he knew that stealin' was wrong.

When th' others complained, the fourth he explained
    That he had a deadly sin.
The three others paled when the preacher unveiled
    That his sin was gossipin'.

Howard Parker
Gordon, Nebraska

Howard is a full-time cattle rancher who has participated in poetry gatherings in eleven of the western states. His work has been included in *Western Horseman, Cowboy Magazine*, and other publications. He won the Nebraska State Rodeo Association saddle bronc championship three times, and says, "While I never made any money at it, I am still proud of the fact." He loves the land he lives on and the people and animals that share it with him.

HORSE TRADIN'

Well, a horse trader he showed up one day,
And he sure would wheel and deal,
For horses, saddles, bridle bits—
Anything he could buy or steal.

And I started thinking about Ol' Pal
And wonderin' what he'd bring.
He was cow-hocked and parrot-mouthed
And he just turned twelve this spring.

And anything that he could do,
He couldn't do too well.
I just happened to have him handy,
Out in the round corral.

Well, the trader takes a look at him,
And Lordy, don't ya know,
He found some other things that's wrong,
That I didn't think would show.

Well, he'd make me an offer,
Then he'd take another chew,
And I'd talk about how dry it was,
And wondered what the hay would do.

Then finally we struck a deal,
Some later in the day.
And I've got the money in my hand
As I watch him pull away.

Then I got to thinkin'
About that ol' horse, ya see;
Wonderin' where he'd end up,
And who his new owner would be.

'Cuz if ya didn't want to rope him,
You better have some oats or corn.
And that ol' devil would still bog his head
On a cold December morn.

Well, they were gonna have an auction,
And it wasn't far away.
And I thought that I would drive over,
Not doin' much that day.

Well, the trader gave his testimony,
With Ol' Pal a-standin' there,
How, "he was plumb safe for anybody,
And you could catch him anywhere."

Then there was a lot of other things
I didn't know that he could do,
Like, "rope calves or steers off him,
Pick up buckin' horses, too!"

So when the biddin' started,
I just got right in the game.
And I guess I didn't know when to stop,
'Cuz the ringman called my name!

Well, I lost two hundred dollars,
But Ol' Pal is mine once more.
At least he's four years younger
Than he was the time before.

A GRASS-FAT STEER
Howard Parker

Well, a bunch of us had gathered at the bar in Cactus Flat,
and talk had turned to cattle and what it takes to get 'em fat.

Some spoke of wheat and barley as the only kind of feed,
while others held for corn, saying that was all you need.

Well, there was this old-timer down there on a corner seat,
and I knew from his past history that he damned near lived
    on meat.

So I went down and asked him what he thought that it would take
for nourishing a critter to produce the finest steak.

He said, "I've eaten every kind of beef produced in this fair land
and there's nothing beats a grass-fat steer wearing someone
    else's BRAND!"

Pat Richardson
Merced, California

Pat has been writing poetry for his own amusement for years but, until recently, he was reluctant to share it with others. He rodeoed in the fifties, riding bulls and saddle broncs, and cartooned for the *Rodeo Sports News*. Of the ranching lifestyle he says, "I like it for the privacy— you're not right next to someone else." Pat currently owns a trucking business and runs a small spread.

STOP ME

"Stop me if you've heard this," the aging cowboy said.
We all tried to stop him, but he went right ahead.

"I drew a palomino horse, weighed fifteen hundred pounds,
I had won the first two days, this was the final round.

"It happened up in Boise, in fifty-two," he said.
"Stan Gomez won the doggin'; he could tell you, but he's dead.

"Dorsey won the ropin', he could verify it's true,
But hell, come to think of it, ol' E. V. is dead, too.

"Dogie Davidson was ridin' bulls, he'll back up my tale,
But I heard someone killed him in a Tijuana jail.

"Nunnemaker seen it, he could say it's so,
But he died of cancer fifteen years ago!

"It's a sorry situation, all my pals have up and died!
But anyway, let's get back to tellin' 'bout my ride."

He paused for several minutes, a strange look on his face.
His eyes had a vacant look as he stared into space.

He'd forgot what he was tellin'; we were kissed by lady luck.
We wouldn't have to listen to that palomino buck.

We'd heard him ride the same horse in pinto and in bay,
Sorrel, and sevina, just depending on the day.

Each time he told it, he added touches here and there,
Sometimes as a gelding, a stud horse, or a mare.

But regardless of the color, the sex, or of the weight,
He rode and spurred it handily, wound up lookin' great.

We all knew he was lyin', every word he said,
'Cause he never told the story till the witnesses were dead.

Jim Ross
Stevensville, Montana

J im was born on a ranch "a long time ago" in the Bull
Mountains of Montana. He has written and published
three books of cowboy poetry and has been a featured
poet at numerous poetry gatherings. Much of his poetry, he
says, "comes from true experiences on the ranch and the rest
'just comes.'"

DEAR DOCTOR (A LETTER)

I sure hate bothering a man like you,
But this cowboy is in an awful stew;
I've not penned a note since my daddy died,
Still my feelings are such that I can't hide.

Since taking Elixer, it's done wonders for me;
There's a glint in my eye, a spring in my knee.
I'm ninety years old and terrible in love;
I so want to marry my turtledove.

She's just twenty-five, a chick of delight,
But I must confess a degree of fright;
My good friends advise that such an engage
Just might prove fatal, this diff'rence in age.

Our affair is torrid; what shall I do?
I'll wait with intent an answer from you;
Please hurry it up, and I will abide,
But we so want to wed; I want a bride.

It wasn't too long there came in the mail
    An envelope posted from Doc MacPhail;
Slim scanned the letter, then read it aloud
    To his concerned friends, that revered crowd.

"Take the Elixer and double the dose,
    Marry the maiden, then hold her real close;
Treat her as equal and query no whys,
    Let nature prevail; if she dies, she dies."

Skinny Rowland
Helena, Montana

Skinny travels all over the West to perform at poetry gatherings, which he enjoys, but says, "I do not know how long I will be able to keep it up as I have ALS (Lou Gehrig's disease) but it will be as long as I can still stand up in front of a mike and make people laugh." Recipient of the Dick Spencer Memorial Award for Outstanding Western Entertainer (an honor given to only three people so far), Skinny writes a regular column for *The Cowboy Magazine* and two other publications. Of his poems he explains, "All of it either comes from experiences or lies, and I haven't had too much experience."

FROM BAD TO WORSE

Now my wife just left and the well went dry,
and my horse is sick and about to die.

Then my still blew up and the barn burned down,
and the road washed out on the way to town.

Then my dog got rabies and bit the cat,
and they both died soon after that.

Now I lost my specs and my pipe stem broke,
so I can't even sit and read and smoke.

Then a tree fell on the chicken shed,
and most of the hens got smashed plumb dead.

Then a chimney fire took half of a wall,
and this old shack is about to fall.

Then I caught my heel on an old dead vine,
and sat smack dab on a porcupine.

Then a beaver dam broke an' my bridge washed out,
and my watch stopped working and I've got the gout.

And the bank foreclosed so I've lost my place,
and my cow disappeared without a trace.

They cut off my credit at the grocery store,
and I lost my job and a whole lot more.

I must have been hexed by a triple curse,
as things keep going from bad to worse.

And now fate has hit me a last dirty crack:
to top off the worst—my wife's coming back.

THE BIG ONE
Skinny Rowland

Now in Montana's Big Hole is where I made fishing history,
and how you could've missed this tale, to me is sure a mystery.

But in a secret spot I know, one day I cast my line;
something grabbed the bait and ran—it made my reel whine.

The pole bent double, the line it snapped, I fought to hold
    my ground,
and then I seen that mighty splash, and my heart began
    to pound.

It was right there on that spot that I became a firm believer
that even a calm guy like myself can catch the fishing fever.

So I got myself a bigger pole and put on my biggest spinner,
but this time he took the pole and all; again he was the winner.

Well, things kept on a-going till I was down to my last hope,
which was a king-sized derrick hook on a three-inch nylon rope.

I dallied around a great big tree and tied to one just like it,
then tossed the hook into the hole and watched that bugger strike it.

I knew I had him hooked for good, but he gave it his best try;
the water churned like a tidal wave, and the hole was near
    splashed dry.

Then in one great mighty effort, he made his final gallant stand;
he made a jump you won't believe, but came down on hard
    dry land.

I can't tell you what his weight was; he was too big for any scale,
but you can rest assured, men, he outweighed the largest whale.

Once there was a feller who claimed he caught the record weight—
well, it was a fish the size of his that was on my hook for bait.

Now no one has caught one bigger, I'll bet you all a buck;
it took a fleet of forklifts just to get it on the truck.

I know there are a few of you who might think this a spoof,
but I have a photograph I took to furnish proof.

I haven't got it with me, but I'll swear the truth abounds;
that fish it was so doggone big, the picture weighs ten pounds.

THE ROAD TO TOWN
Skinny Rowland

Now that old road out to the ranch, it needs a little repair;
it has some ruts along the way and a pothole here and there.

Now a time or two while riding, I couldn't tell which was which,
so I picked out the better part, and rode home in the ditch.

Well, then the road was better, and now it's worse, of course;
the last time I tried to use it, I high-centered my doggone horse.

Now the preacher came to visit, but somewheres along the way,
he jumped in time to save his life, but that road sucked up his shay.

The sheriff lost his buckboard, and the doctor lost his surrey;
my wife has gone and not returned, so my team is cause for worry.

Last week came a dun for taxes, so I told them not to fret it,
but just to hook a buggy up and come on out and get it.

So now this week a ranger came, along with a federal inspector,
looking for a horse and rig and a missing tax collector.

Well, even then considering things, it was time to fix that road,
and put some gravel here and there, at least a wheelbarrow load.

But I've postponed that chore now; there's a more convenient day.
My mother-in-law just sent a wire; she's planning to come and stay.

Dakota Slim
Sturgis, South Dakota

Dakota Slim is retired from ranching, but not from cowboy poetry. He attends several gatherings every year, getting ideas for poems from his own experiences and those described to him by others. He has published books of his poetry, noting that he didn't start typing until he was seventy years old.

OLD COWS

We retired into town
With beautiful flowers all aroun'.
The garden club came to see what's done—
How our little place was run,

Why our flowers were big and green—
There must be something that can't be seen.
They wanted to know what process
Was the secret of our success.

My wife said, "To make flowers mature
I just use old cow manure.
Old cow manure is better than most
And sure beats trying to make compost."

There was a snobbish little miss
Who looked puzzled as she asked this,
"Old cow manure? Oh! I see,
But just how old should that cow be?"

JUST THIRSTY
Dakota Slim

I had just come out of Nebraska
And was riding in the Badlands heat.
My horse was slowly walking;
Both of us were really beat.

The devil had turned the heat up;
He was getting us ready for slaughter,
'Cause we had been going all day
Without a drink of water.

The hills looked bleak and barren;
There wasn't a green blade of grass.
The heat waves kept moving the skyline,
But there was a place that looked like a pass.

As we came around a bend,
I squinted ahead in a hot breeze.
I didn't know, but I thought I saw
A green cottonwood and some cedar trees.

Then I saw a tub and a water pump
And a little run-down shack,
And some colorful quilted blankets
On a rickety fence out back.

Then I heard a dog a-barking.
A woman came to the door.
She said, "Howdy, stranger,"
Then at her dog she swore.

Tobacco juice ran down her jaws,
Her teeth were rotten snags,
Her hair was matted and snarled,
And under her eyes were dark bags.

But I asked her for some water.
This situation isn't quite the worst.
There is only one thing badder,
And that is dying of thirst.

She said, "Sure enough. Go down to the pump.
But that pump will need a prime.
Here—I'll do it for you.
You men miss it all the time."

So she took a little can of water—
On top floated a bunch of flies.
She dumped it in and started pumping;
Up came some water, to my surprise.

She looked quite proud at getting water;
Shifted her quid and downed a grasshopper neat.
I guess it would have died anyway
For there was nothing for it to eat.

Now there was a dipper at the fence,
But the tobacco and teeth made me think:
If I took a drink from that dipper,
Would I be able to hold down that drink?

She smiled at me as she filled the dipper.
Now I didn't want to hurt her pride,
So I gulped down the whole dipperful,
But I drank it from the handle side.

So she pumped water for my horse.
She laughed and was happy as can be.
She slapped me on my shoulder and said,
"You drink out a dipper just like me."

HOSS TRADER
Dakota Slim

I was headed for Wyoming,
Just my old hoss and me.
But I got to thinking as how
My hoss ain't what it used to be.

About that time, I saw a sign.
"We trade horses, sell, or buy."
I thought I had nothing to lose.
I'd stop and see this guy.

His horses circled around the corral;
The buckskin was ahead of the rest.
I asked if I could saddle it up
And give that hoss a test.

His teeth were good; his eyes were clear,
And his feet were sound.
My ride on him was smooth as silk,
And he could really cover ground.

The way this hoss ran and turned,
He would really be great for the range.
With a touch of a rein or a press of my knee,
He would turn on a dime and leave change.

I thought I oughter trade.
I'd start low, of course.
So I said, "I'll give you eleven dollars,
And trade you for my good horse."

But he said, "It's a deal!"
So I bought this horse for a song.
I got to thinking how cheap he was;
There really must be something wrong.

Now if this hoss had any defects,
They surely must be hidden,
'Cause I just felt like I was part of him;
It was the best hoss I've ever ridden.

Later, I was getting well along in Wyoming,
When suddenly the buckskin went insane.
I couldn't get it to follow the road;
He wanted to go up a ranch house lane.

After he circled several times,
I decided to give him the rein.
He whirled around and went trotting
Up to the ranch house on the lane.

He stopped and paused a moment,
Then went a-trotting back
And started going up the road;
The reins—they still were slack.

So I rode a couple miles up the road
Until I came to another lane.
That buckskin done the same darn thing,
But why, I couldn't explain.

So when I got to the Bar X Ranch,
(That was the place I was going),
A cowpoke asked, "Where'd you get that horse?"
I was proud of this hoss flesh I was showing.

"That buckskin is sure a beauty.
I vouch for it; I know I can,
'Cause I really know your hoss—
It belonged to our last mailman!"

Marie W. Smith
Somers, Montana

Marie was born in Australia and spent many years ranching in Idaho and Montana. She says she's "retired from being a wife and mom" and has participated in many poetry gatherings, publishing her poetry in several books and magazines. Her eleven children encourage her writing.

A Cowboy's Lunch

I didn't know until I married one,
That cowboys don't pack a lunch;
At least, no self-respecting buckaroo
Would be caught dead with sandwich and punch

If he's riding range to hunt for strays
Or dogies or just herding a bunch
Of wild Texas steers like we bought in the drought,
Helped part of the Lone Star out of a crunch.

So for breakfast I cook sausage and hash browns
And three eggs, yokes broke and fried hard,
My creamed oatmeal and fancy spiced peaches
I can from the tree in the yard,

And gravy and buttermilk biscuits, syrup
And pancakes, honeydew brown,
Until I am sure my cowboy can exist
'Til he gets back way after sundown.

Even though the meal seems substantial,
I worry when noon rolls around
And wish he was closer to fix him
A picnic we can spread on the ground.

But I respect this strange cowboy reasoning,
Think my man has a will of steel,
'Til one day I bake oatmeal cookies
To serve with the evening meal.

"My favorite cookies," my cowboy says,
And he polishes off quite a few.
"Maybe I'll take some tomorrow,"
He smiles, "just to remind me of you."

Now, they are full of nourishment,
Like oatmeal and raisins and nuts
And orange peel and cranberries
And eggs and flour and such.

"I thought cowboys didn't eat any lunch,"
I say next morning as he takes a whole pile.
"Aw, this ain't real food, just somethin' to chaw,"
He says with a crooked smile.

I watch him tuck them out of sight
In his slickered roll of yellow.
"But you don't tell no one, you promise me?"
I nodded. "They wouldn't understand a fella

"Who loves his wife so much that he
Would break the cowboy code."
Whoever had such a loving man?
I think, as I wave him on up the road.

So I always see there are cookies
Made of oatmeal, raisins and nuts,
So my cowboy has something to remember me by,
Though he'll swear he never eats lunch.

COWBOY VERNACULAR
Marie W. Smith

Now, this young school-age cowboy
   still had a couple of years
to finish learning English
   so he could graduate with his peers.

He was like most all the cowboys
   that I have ever met.
He'd say "knowed" for knew and "ain't" for isn't,
   and for "have gone" he'd say he'd went.

This day, his teacher had had enough
   of this "gone" and "went" at school
and said, "Right at three you stay today
   'til you learn this golden rule:

"That there's no need to say 'I have went'
   when you want to say 'I've gone'."
He thought, it's them haves and hads and hases
   that can turn a fella wrong.

So the teacher set the young cowboy
   an after-school assignment—
One hundred lines of "I have gone home"
   on the blackboard as a reminder

That proper English is a must
   if he wanted a diploma.
He'd have to learn the right from wrong,
   that sometimes "went" is a misnomer.

So he stood before the blackboard.
   He wore out several sticks of chalk.
His hand grew cramped, his fingers stiff;
   at eighty-six he began to balk.

He moved back, surveyed his work—
   Eighty-six was quite a sum.
"I have wrote eighty-six lines," he signed,
   "and now I have went home."

THE DANCE
Marie W. Smith

I asked this crusty cowboy
How he had met his future wife,
And he settled with eyes a-twinkling
To tell me something of his life.

"How did I meet my lady love?
Why, I met her face to face
One balmy summer evening
At the dance at Timkin's place.

"'Course that was many years ago,
When I was punchin' cows
For Barney Gill, the Irishman,
Whose wife was always at me as hows

"I oughta take a wife and raise
Some kids, so's I'd be proud
To see my own posterity
Before I was in the ground.

"So's I promised Barney's little wife,
Even though I was scairt o'girls,
That I'd go next week to Timkin's place,
Give this courtin' thing a whirl.

"Now, Charley Timkin's brand new wife
Had asked a friend up from the city,
An' I had heard the bunkhouse talk
How it was a terrible pity

"That some upright, upstandin' hand
Didn't step to an' take a chance
An' do some princely courtin'
On Saturday at the dance.

"Well, I was the only single one,
So's I knowed what they was suggestin',
An' it was so distressin' to me
I come down with indigestion.

"Now, pretty Mrs. Timkins,
She was prim 'n' proper, too,
Had demanded there be some changes made—
Had even painted the cranny blue.

"Now, it was a new two-holer
That for the convenience of the sexes,
Charley had been persuaded
To partition into two spaces.

"So he built a flimsy, pinewood wall,
Put another door on the side near the fence,
An' painted the signs real pretty.
They said 'Ladies' on one, and 'Gents'.

"Well, Saturday, I spiffed myself
As best as I could handle.
I spit on my boots 'n' everything,
But my nerves, they was quite a jangle.

"I wanted to get up closer
To this gorgeous city lady;
Maybe ask her to dance a bit,
But it's hell to be shy and jady.

"Then I sees her sidle out the door
An' I thinks that 'now's my chance',
So I licks my hair back down a bit
An' takes a hitch up on my pants.

"But then when I gets outside,
I sees she's not just come out for air,
But she's headed for the cranny
To spend a moment there.

"Well, I waits outside for quite a while,
So long I almost got the bends.
So as quietly as possible
I went through the door marked 'Gents'.

"I did the usual things that's done
During a visit such as this
An' strained my ears to hear
If she was through, this city miss.

"I tried to be real quiet
So's not to embarrass her or me,
An' pretty soon I reckoned that
She must there no longer be.

"Just to be positively certain,
I buttoned up my pants and stood,
Then decided I should check for sure
An' put my head down on the wood.

"Though I didn't exactly relish
My head in the hole in that place,
I did, an' that's how it happened:
I met my missus face to face."

Red Steagall
Fort Worth, Texas

Red Steagall has been a songwriter, recording artist, and television and motion picture personality for over twenty-five years. He is perhaps best known for his Texas Swing dance music and the many songs he has written. In 1991, the Texas Legislature named him the official Cowboy Poet of Texas.

THE PICTURE

The little frame house in the cottonwood trees
Looks the same as when I was a kid.
I slept on the porch on those hot summer nights,
Because that's what my grandfather did.

Grandpa was a cowboy, my hero and friend,
And I thought he was twenty foot tall.
I dogged out his footsteps from morning till night,
Then I went back to school in the fall.

He worked on the Matador when he was young,
And the Four 6's Panhandle branch.
He came back to Weatherford, married Grandma,
And they bought this old hardscrabble ranch.

Each day was a struggle; they somehow got by,
Tho' the banker owned most of their stock.
They raised longhorn cows and a houseful of kids
On mesquite brush and cedar and rock.

His old spinster sister has just passed away,
And she left me a bunch of her stuff.
A big box of pictures of him and Grandma,
And a case of four dot Garrett snuff.

I drove out this morning to show them these things
And identify all of my kin,
So they become people with faces and names,
Like a cousin or old family friend.

Grandma was tickled and she knew every face.
She'd name 'em and I'd write 'em down.
Grandpa in his rocker just fooled with his hat;
He kept changing the crease in the crown.

Was one in particular she studied hard.
It was her and Grandpa on this place.
Her calico dress was a sign of the times,
And his hat covered most of his face.

Dry cowhides were hanging across the top rail.
That's all they had left from the drought.
She said, "Look here, Pa, you remember, this year
Was the summer we nearly pulled out."

He put on his glasses and laid down his hat,
Then he stared at the picture awhile.
He squinted his eyes and then looked up at her,
And he answered in true cowboy style.

"That black bald-faced pony, why, that's Curly Wolf,
That renegade, jugheaded runt.
The stockin'-legged pony is old Santy Claus.
But, Ma, who are these people in front?"

Colen H. Sweeten, Jr.
Malad City, Idaho

A veteran of World War II, Colen spent the early years of his life on a grain and livestock ranch in southern Idaho "before trucks, combines, squeeze chutes, and gooseneck horse trailers." He has published three booklets and one tape, and enjoys the ranching lifestyle because "you can feel you are your own boss and can make your own decisions in doing the thing you enjoy doing."

COW ON THE FIGHT

This happens a lot to a cowman,
You can nod if I'm tellin' it right.
You're never ignored and surely not bored,
When you get an old cow on the fight.

Some people may think it is funny,
And cowboys on the fence always laugh.
But it's never a joke when you are the poke
Caught between the cow and her calf.

Oh, a cowboy is brave when he's mounted
On a good horse, with his rope and his spurs.
But when he's dancin' in dust with a cow he can't trust,
The advantage is definitely hers.

You dismount to play doctor out on the range,
And your kindness turns into a fight.
Then you start lookin' 'round from there on the ground,
And your horse is nowhere in sight.

Your legs know what to do (and they do it, too!)
With her hot breath on the back of your neck.
Do you know how it feels to have spurs on your heels,
And racin' downhill to a wreck?

Cowboys get jitters when workin' those critters,
Without a horse to keep 'em up in the air.
And if your luck is like mine, it's just a matter of time
'Til she's wipin' her nose on your hair.

Someone has to step down when there's work on the ground,
But to volunteer doesn't make any sense.
The worst part of the job, is the grinnin'-faced mob
Lined up on the pole of the fence.

While I'm takin' a lickin' from hookin' and kickin',
They yell and they cheer for the cow!
I've limped and I've bled and got kicked in the head,
And they're not even satisfied now.

That old brockle-faced roan is very well known.
And I tell you she's nobody's pet.
So I told the boys who make all the noise,
I'd introduce her to the vet.

While the vet put on his apron, she ripped off my shirt,
And we both went around and around.
I just couldn't see with both eyes full of dirt,
And I wound up huggin' the ground.

Bein' pressed into the dirt didn't much hurt,
And then my ribs caved in with a pop.
It's no fun at all when you're the first one to fall,
And that ornery old cow is on top!

Then she went on by and left me to die,
I could feel warm blood comin' out of my ear.
I reached up and touched it with the arm that still worked,
As the heifer dust started to clear.

But the blood wasn't red, it was more of a brown,
And it carried a terrible smell.
Them fence-sittin' cowboys and that brockle-faced roan
Can every last one go to hell!

WORKING VACATION
Colen H. Sweeten, Jr.

I found the answer to my boredom
In the classified ad that I read;
"We'll give you a working vacation"—
That's just what the paper said.

Well, I didn't know about dude ranches
And you might think that is strange,
But I had spent my lifetime
Working out there on the range.

The man in the government office
Said I could go out and earn some dough,
And they wouldn't deduct it from my pension,
Like when I worked four years ago.

So I gassed up the truck and rolled my bed
And bought a map to show the way,
And Monday morning I hit that ranch
At just about the break of day.

I got the job without question—
I was the only cowboy that showed.
They didn't ask about experience
Or about the horses I had rode.

The boss took my name and address,
Said, "You are on 'til Sunday night."
I should have been suspicious when he said,
"Will nine hundred be all right?"

I didn't understand but I nodded
When I should have made a correction.
I was on the right track but, alas and alack,
I was headed the wrong direction.

They gave me an old pony to straddle,
A pinto with one gimpy knee.
Then I spent every day in the saddle
Ridin' horses that were older than me.

Sunday night I went to the office
As the sunset was touching the hill;
The boss came out with some papers,
And the "paycheck" I got was a bill!

Well, I paid the man nine hundred dollars;
I felt as stupid as one of his mules.
I'd like one more chance at savin' the ranch
If I could play with this new set of rules!

I'd hire on double the cowboys;
They could sit in the shade of a tree.
I wouldn't care if they worked or not
As long as they were paying me.

We'd have three meals a day in the big house
With tablecloths whiter than snow,
A white-aproned cook with a mustache,
And every evening there'd be a big show.

I thought about this newfangled idea;
There were many good points I could see.
I could cut overhead and save the spread
With all the help payin' money to me.

Somehow I envy that outfit
And the rancher who is using his head.
The cold and the heat and the low price of meat
Will never cause him to give up his spread.

SEEING RED

Colen H. Sweeten, Jr.

Trailing cattle on the highway
Is not what it used to be,
And riding drag on a gentle old nag
Is not where I'd choose to be.

But the boys said, "Grandpa, you've had it,
But you still like to hang around.
So if you don't mind, we'll let you ride behind
And help slow the traffic down."

Cripples and lame and lazy,
And one bull with a gimpy knee,
Worn-out calves and stragglers
Was all I could hope to see.

Pretty soon here comes a sports car,
Brand new and candy-apple red.
"That kid's sure in a hurry,"
I shook my head and said.

He sat that new car up real hard
With some squeelin' of the wheels,
But he misjudged a little bit
And he bumped that old bull's heels.

The bull had been on green feed
And I guess he'd filled up pretty good,
He jumped ahead, left his breakfast spread
Across the top of that red hood.

The windshield was all splattered
And mixed in with the dust.
The wipers spread it back and forth
Like peanut butter on a crust.

"Oh, what a shame, I'm sorry,
I'd clean it off," I said,
"But that would not be safe right now
With that car that's solid red."

"Red brings out the beast in cows,
And it's twice as bad with bulls.
I'm afraid he'll bring his horns back here
And punch this new car full of holes."

I quickly moved my horse aside
To look for a safer place.
That car spun around and hit for town;
You should have seen that feller's face.

I think I'll sign on for this job
When they trail 'em home next fall;
Ridin' drag on this gentle old nag
Is not so boring after all.

Charles Williams
Dallas, Texas

A professional storyteller for over ten years, Charles works days as an engineer for a large electronics firm. However, he enjoys the ranching/rural lifestyle for "the inner strength it gives you." He grew up on a farm in New York and spent the first two decades of his life "working cows (dairy, not beef), tractors (not horses), and other livestock (pigs, chickens, and sheep), but 'Ride 'em Pigboy' just doesn't have that ring to it."

ROUGH ROAD BILL

Now, Rough Road Bill was a tough old coot—
A range-ridin', cow-chasin', hard-drinkin' galoot.
He'd spent his whole life somewhere out on the range;
Some said he was crazy, others, "Just a little strange."

He'd been through it all, the good an' the bad,
The wrecks an' roundups, the glad times an' sad.
He'd right honest come by his name—Rough Road Bill,
But I reckon his worst break came on Polecat Hill.

He'd been out skylarkin' an' got bit, ya see,
By a rabid coon he'd roped out of a tree.
By the time he got in to see the Doc,
Them fatal words was a terrible shock.

The sawbones told him there weren't no hope,
Hydrophoby'd gone through him at a lope.
As soon as he heard the bleak odds he was fightin',
Old Bill grabbed a paper an' started to writin'.

Then Doc says, "You got a few days left, Bill,
To finish off the writin' of your will."
Bill growled, "This ain't no will I got to write—
Naw, it's a list o' the people I'm a'-goin' ta bite."

Perry L. Williams
Lubbock, Texas

Perry owns a real estate appraisal company and has a small livestock operation. He has participated in several cowboy poetry gatherings and even recited poetry on a television commercial for Roy Rogers' Restaurants. He says that "several years on the rodeo circuit as a bull rider and rodeo clown kinda fine-tuned my ability to find humor in some of the worst of situations!"

DININ' OUT

Tex went down to the feedstore
And signed up to win a trip
To leave out of Houston, Texas,
On a leaky sailin' ship.

Well, shore enough his name got drawed
For a trip to New York City,
Where there weren't too many cowboys,
But they said the girls were pretty.

And Tex had always wanted to
Do other things, as well,
Like order up a fancy meal
At a shore first-class hotel.

'Cause he'd always heard the Waldorf-
Astoria was the best.
So he ordered up a T-bone steak
To put 'em to the test.

"Yes, sir," the stuffy waiter said
As he acts somewhat discreet
And turns his nose up when he sees
What's on the cowboy's feet.

Heck, Ol' Tex had on his workin' boots,
All scuffed and showin' wear,
Boots that's seen a heap of wearin'
But seen very little care.

So the prissy waiter went on back
And turned the order in.
Then 'fore Tex could catch his breath
The guy was back again.

He said, "I've brought your soup, sir,"
And with very little tact
He set the bowl in front of Tex,
But Tex, he shoved 'er back

And said he didn't order soup,
That he had ordered meat;
Sent it back into the kitchen
'Cause it wudn't fit to eat.

But the waiter come back with the soup,
Said, "The cook's some mad, no doubt."
So Tex, he says, "Forget it,"
Grabs his hat and storms right out.

So about the time that Tex gets back
To his room, the guy next door
Has a fit and falls a-kickin'
In the middle of the floor.

Well, they calls this lady doctor
Who says no need to worry,
Then prescribes a soothing enema
To be brought up in a hurry!

So these two husky hombres
Go to Tex's room by mistake
And said he didn't have no choice—
That an enema, he'd take.

And proceeded to administer
What Doc said would make him better.
Told Tex to do what he was told
Or it sure 'nuff would upset 'er.

Well, fin'ly Tex, he makes it home
And the boys all want to know
About New York and the things he seen
And the places he did go.

Well, Ol' Tex, he just ignores 'em
And don't have much to say.
But they just keep on a-pesterin'
Through the night and through the day.

So fin'ly, Tex, he loosens up,
Says, "I'll give you guys some poop.
If you ever dine at the Waldorf, boys,
   . . . BE SURE TO EAT YOUR SOUP!"

No Contest
Perry L. Williams

She woke up 'long about midnight
When she heard her doggie snore,
Then again, at 2:00 A.M.,
When he cut loose with some more.

She said, "I just cain't take this,
Some sleep I've got to get."
So she hauled him in next mornin',
And she took him to the vet.

Well, she charged into the office,
Sayin', "Doc, what can I do?
I just don't get no sleep at all.
He snores the whole night through."

So the Doc, he checks old Fido,
Then he looks her in the eye,
Says, "I shore can't tell for certain,
But there's somethin' you might try.

"Just take a piece of ribbon
And tie around his nose
To cut down on vibration
As that air he huffs and blows."

So she went back to the ranch house,
Found a piece of bright red ribbon
To see if that vet was speakin' truth,
Or if he was a-fibbin'.

Shore enough, it cut the snorin' down,
And she finally got some quiet
'Til along just after midnight,
When she got a little fright.

See, her husband, Pete, come staggerin' in,
As drunk as he could be,
And fell down there across the bed—
Commenced to snorin', don't you see.

Well, she'd put the quiet on Fido,
But all the ribbon left was blue.
So she tied a piece 'round old Pete's nose,
And by gosh, he got quiet, too!

So Pete woke up next mornin',
Saw blue ribbon on his nose,
Then saw ribbon hung on Fido—
'Twas bright red, just like a rose.

Pete says, "I don't know what we got into,
But we did some good, I reckon.
'Cause whatever it was, I see, old pard,
. . . That we came in first and second!"

THE COOK-OFF
Perry L. Williams

They circled up the wagons and
Got ready for the test.
See, the cowboy cooks was fixin'
To find out who was best.

And what a motley-lookin' bunch
Of hombres they did make
When they set up there in Lubbock
And proceeded in to bake

Cowboy biscuits cooked in style,
And beans that tasted great,
With slow-cooked meat that smelled so good
That folks could hardly wait

For judges to get through markin'
All them points down on their sheet.
Why, it was gettin' close to twelve o'clock,
And time for us to eat.

See, one judge said, "This wagon here,
I like their biscuits best."
But the second judge thought X-Bar's beans
Were better than the rest.

So the third judge says, "Those are good beans,
Biscuits baked the way they should,
But my favorite is the brisket,
Slow-cooked on prairie wood."

Well, the judges just could not agree,
And the time began to fly.
So they decided on a cook-off
Of a shore 'nuff cowboy pie.

So Dago Red starts in to cookin',
But he don't know what to fix.
Then he gets a great idea
And pours Jack Daniels in his mix.

Well, the judges starts to eatin',
And they really do get mellow,
And all agree that Dago Red's
A top-notch cookin' fellow.

But this makes the others mad enough
To make the score cards fly—
'Til they all got tame as little lambs
  . . . after tastin' Dago's pie.

IT AIN'T NECESSARILY SO

Perry L. Williams

A man from Czechoslovakia,
He came to Dallas town
And asked a broke young cowboy
To show him all around.

The cowboy says, "I would, ole pard,
But I ain't got a buck.
No groceries in the kitchen,
No gas in my old truck."

"Oh, I see," the tourist feller says,
"So I'll tell you what I'll do.
Just show me this here Dallas town,
And I'll do good things for you—

"Like pay you money for your time,
Even rent a fancy car,
Pay the bills when we do go into
A cafe or a bar."

So the man from Czechoslovakia
And the cowboy make a deal
To go and see the sights in town,
With the cowboy at the wheel.

Since the cowboy he's new in town,
He didn't know what to do.
But he finally figured where to go—
He'd just take 'im to the zoo.

They drove up to the zoo park.
The Czech bought the tickets there,
Then said to this young cowboy,
"Let's go see the grizzly bear."

Well, shore 'nuff, they finally found 'em
And walked up to the cage,
Where they found not one, but two big bears,
And both were in a rage.

So this gent from Czechoslovakia
Gets close to see the dark one's hide
When what happens, but one grabs him up
And pulls him right inside.

Then right before the cowboy's eyes,
The bear eats him in one bite.
Why, the man from Czechoslovakia
Disappears plumb out of sight!

Well, the zoo men they come runnin',
Found the cowboy lookin' frail.
They ask which bear had got 'im.
The cowboy said, "It was the male."

So the vet he drugged old poppa bear,
And just like a good Boy Scout,
Says, "I'll do an operation, men,
To get that hombre out."

He cut through skin and muscle,
Reached and pulled back all that hair,
Took a quick look and discovered
He had skinned the wrong darned bear.

Now the moral of this story, friend,
And seldom will it fail:
Don't always believe it when a cowboy says,
" . . . the Czech is in the male!"

ACKNOWLEDGMENTS

Virginia Bennett, "Nice Work If You Can Get It," "Storms on the Divide," and "Hazards of Bragging" were previously published in *Legacy of the Land*, 1993.

Ed Brown, "Bronc Rides," and "More Shorter" were previously published in *Rhyme Doesn't Pay*, 1987.

Elizabeth Ebert, "The Cemetery" was previously published in *Grand River Tales & Other Poems*, 1991. "The Last Great Rabbit Hunt" was previously published in *Trails to Thunder Hawk*, 1992.

Peggy Godfrey, "Get It Right, Fella!" was previously published in *Write 'Em Roughshod*, 1994. "Sellin' Postholes" was previously published in *Write 'Em Cowboy*, 1993.

Tony Illardi, "Old Joker" and "The Dead Horse" were previously published in *Adventure West* magazine.

Bill Jones, "Little Slim" was previously published in *There Ain't Much Romance in the Life of Us Cows*, and *Cattle, Horses, Grass & Sky*. "The Pretzel Hold" was previously published in *The Pretzel Hold*. "The Cook's Revenge" was previously published in the 1993 *Western Horseman* cowboy calendar and *There Ain't Much Romance in the Life of Us Cows*.

Phil Kennington, "The Cowboy and the Seagull," "Rocket," "The Lost Cow," "A Cowboy Goes to Town," "The Skunk and the Cowboys," "Cowboy Granola," and "Shotgun Chaps" were all previously published in *Horse Sense*.

John "Jay" Kulm, "A Giant Four-Point Buck" was previously published in *American Cowboy Poet* magazine, 1991.

Mike Logan, "Cowboy Cruise Control" was previously published in *Men of the Open Range and Other Poems*, by Mike Logan.

Wayne Nelson, "Snowville" was previously published in *Dry Crik Review*.

Chip O'Brien, "Skinny Evans" was previously published in *Downwind O' Cows*. "Four Preachers Confessin'" was previously published in *The Outhouse Reader*.

Marie W. Smith, "A Cowboy's Lunch" was previously published in *The Cowboy Poetry Cookbook*, Gibbs Smith, Publisher, 1992. "Cowboy Vernacular" was previously published in *North & East of Down Under*. "The Dance" was previously published in *North & East of Down Under*, and *Dry Crik Review*.

Colen H. Sweeten, Jr., "Cow on the Fight" was previously published in *Cowboy Poetry*, 1987. "Working Vacation" was previously published in *Back at the Ranch*, 1992 (both books by Colen H. Sweeten, Jr.).